ECHOES FROM
PATMOS

A Study of Revelation

by

Bishop Ronald Wilson

I pray this book will be
A blessing to you!
Best Wishes
Ronald

Romans 15:13

Bishop Ronald Wilson

and Marlene Wilson

From the Author

My study of the Book of Revelation began shortly after I accepted Jesus as my personal Savior. While others have spent considerable time debating the vague personages and images of this book, that has never been my focus. The list of renowned scholars who have attempted to explain these entities is a lengthy one, and even the most casual reading will soon reveal that even they have numerous disagreements. In the midst of what we may never understand on this earth, there are some of the greatest truths and teachings of the Bible. That has always been the heart of my study as you will find in reading this book. Recently, I have been encouraged to publish my notes. During all these years of study, I never considered the possibility of publishing my research. But, now it is done.

Please Note:

➤ The Appendix of this publication provides a list of literature that has been a resource for me over the years.

➤ Scriptural quotes in this book are from the King James Version of the Bible. All Punctuation, language style and spelling of Scriptural quotes reflect the KJV.

➤ A special thanks to Amelia Billingsley who has served as Editorial and Publication Assistant for this book.

CONTENTS

I. Introduction   1

II. The Revelation   3

III. The Seven Churches   13

IV. The Great and Terrible Day
      of the Lord   87

V. Chapters 4-22   91

VI. Appendix   203

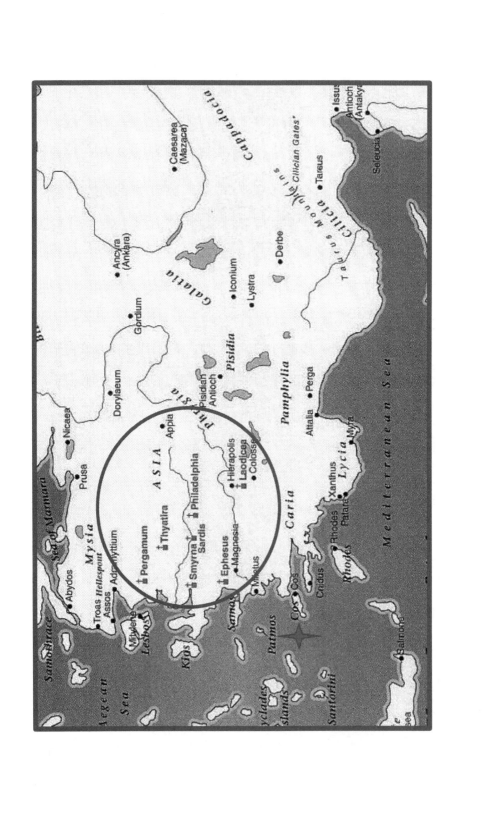

Echoes from Patmos

I

Introduction

The entire Bible is a book about Jesus. Taking Jesus out of the Bible is like removing the stars from the heavens. The curtain rises in Genesis and descends in Revelation. In between the two, we have the incredible story of God dealing with humanity. Sin is the conflict, and redemption is the theme.

Reading the book of Revelation is like reading the final chapter of a 2,000 page novel. To understand the final chapter, one must connect it with the chapters that come before. Nearly all the imagery and events the reader encounters in Revelation are introduced earlier in books such as Ezekiel, Daniel, Zechariah, Matthew, Thessalonians and Peter. All of these will be referenced in our study. We begin with a brief summary of the book of Revelation.

It is the book of the Revelation of Jesus Christ. Jesus was present in Genesis chapter 1, and we see a promise concerning Him in Genesis, chapter 3. Revelation shows His completed work.

We see the Church, those who heeded the call to come out from the world to become the family of God. It speaks of the resurrection of the saints. There are only two sets of people in the world. The saints, and the "ain'ts" -- those who are in the family of God and those who "ain't", if you will pardon my grammar.

We are given graphic details of the Great Tribulation, that seven-year period that is missing in chapter 9 of Daniel and that period which the prophets refer to as the great and dreadful day of the Lord. All of that comes to a completion in Revelation.

We see the serpent of Genesis chapter 3 and the final defeat of evil. We also get a glimpse of who the devil was prior to the creation account. These were recorded in Isaiah 14 and Ezekiel 28. All of that is uncovered in Revelation.

The Antichrist, who is part of an unholy trinity, will be a key character in the last days. We see the end of apostate Christianity, or perhaps a better way of saying that is, "those who pretended to be Christian but never were".

Details about the second coming of Christ are in this book. And then, finally, we see the ultimate fulfillment of the promise that God made in the Garden of Eden and the Covenant that God made with Abraham and his descendants (The children of Israel, who are God's chosen people, as well as all who have accepted Jesus Christ as their Savior.) All of this comes together and finds its ultimate completion in the book of Revelation.

II
The Revelation

Revelation 1:1, "The Revelation of Jesus Christ, which God gave unto Him, to shew unto His servants, things which must shortly come to pass."

The word "Revelation" in the original Greek is "apokálypsis." The word literally means, "to take off the veil; to reveal." By its very definition, the book of Revelation is not meant to be mysterious. It is meant to be understood. So, what is it about? The very first verse tells us that the book is an unveiling of those things which must shortly come to pass.

It was around the year 95 AD that Jesus revealed these things in Revelation to the Apostle John. John was the last living Apostle. James, the brother of John, was the first Apostle to be martyred, but of the original 12 now only John remains.

During the reign of Caesar Nero, there was unrestricted persecution against the Church and countless thousands of Christians were slaughtered. When Nero died, the persecution subsided somewhat until Domitian became Caesar in 81 A.D. While most Christians have at least heard of Nero, few recognize the name Domitian. In truth, Domitian made Nero look like a choir boy. The persecution under Domitian was so bad that those early Christians thought they must surely be living in the last days.

If you read the writings of both Peter and Paul, you can sense that they know they are about to die, but Jesus hasn't returned. They really thought they would live to see His return. Peter seems to have settled that question in his mind this way. In 2 Peter 3, he realized that if you are God, and you have eternity past behind you, and you have eternity future before you, time becomes irrelevant. A thousand years is like a day, and a day is like a thousand years. Time for God is not like time for us.

2 Peter 3:8-10, "(8) But, beloved, be not ignorant of this one thing, that one day is with the Lord as a thousand years, and a thousand years as one day. (9) The Lord is not slack concerning His promise, as some men count slackness; but is longsuffering to us-ward, not willing that any should perish, but that all should come to repentance. (10) But the day of the Lord will come as a thief in the night; in the which the heavens shall pass away with a great noise, and the elements shall melt with fervent heat, the earth also and the works that are therein shall be burned up."

James 5:7 tells us that God is being patient so that as many as possible can be saved. "Be patient therefore, brethren, unto the coming of the Lord. Behold, the husbandman waiteth for the precious fruit of the earth, and hath long patience for it, until He receive the early and latter rain." The question that many are asking is simply this; how much longer will it be until Jesus returns?

Revelation 1:4, "John to the seven churches which are in Asia: grace be unto you, and peace, from Him which is, and which was, and which is to come; and from the seven Spirits which are before His throne."

After the day of Pentecost, the early Christians initially met in homes. On Paul's second missionary journey, he visited Ephesus and seems to have been the one who officially organized the church there. (Acts 18:19) But Christianity was already established in Ephesus before Paul arrived. In Acts 2, on the day of Pentecost, there were people in Jerusalem who were from that area. They went back home carrying the Good News of the Gospel. Paul would later return and spend two years teaching in Ephesus. (Acts 19:8-10)

With the passing of time, trouble arose in Ephesus prompting Paul to send Timothy to help restore order. Later, according to Church tradition, the Apostle John went to Ephesus and became pastor. It appears that John served as the pastor of Ephesus before he was exiled to Patmos and again after he was released from Patmos. Remember this because it takes on great significance when we look closely at each of the churches in Revelation.

If you look at the map, you will see that the other six churches were also within reach of John's influence. By today's standard of transportation, all were within a few hours drive from Ephesus.

A timeline is established. Revelation 1:4-8, "From Him which is; (the present;) which was; (the past,) and which is to come; (the future.") From Jesus Christ, Who is the faithful witness, and the first begotten of the dead, and the Prince of the kings of the earth. Unto Him that loved us and washed us from our sins in His own blood, and hath made us kings and priests unto God and His Father; to Him be glory and dominion for ever and ever. Amen. Behold, He cometh with clouds; and every eye shall see Him, and they also which pierced Him: and all kindreds of the earth shall wail because of Him. Even so, Amen." These verses reference Zechariah chapter 14.

Verse 8, "I am Alpha and Omega, the beginning and the ending, saith the Lord, which is, and which was, and which is to come, the Almighty." There are our three time periods again; present, past and future, reminding us that God is eternal, He is from everlasting to everlasting.

Verse 9 focuses our attention briefly on John. "I John, who also am your brother, and companion in tribulation, and in the kingdom and patience of Jesus Christ, was in the isle that is called Patmos, for the Word of God, and for the testimony of Jesus Christ."

It was mentioned previously how the persecution of Christians dramatically escalated under Domitian. John was the last living Apostle. Imagine how much they would like to have arrested John, put him on trial and then executed him. But what would you accomplish by executing a 90 to 95-year-old man? It would have created a martyr of epic proportions.

Realizing that this would be a terrible mistake, John was instead arrested and exiled to the prison island of Patmos. Look again at the map and see that Patmos is southwest of Ephesus, in the Aegean Sea. The idea was that if John could be removed from interacting with the people, this new faith would just fizzle out. Don't kill him, just banish him and remove his influence from the whole movement. This is what they thought, but little did they realize that they had strategically banished John to a place where God would give him a great revelation.

When most people think about the book of Revelation, they think almost exclusively about "the things which are yet to be." But the first three chapters are vitally important because they lay a foundation and issue both approvals and warnings to the churches that existed then and will continue to exist until the return of the Lord. It is this foundation that gives validity to the rest of the book.

Revelation 1:10-11, "I was in the Spirit on the Lord's day, and heard behind me a great voice, as of a trumpet, saying, I am Alpha and Omega, the first and the last: and, What thou seest, write in a book, and send it unto the seven churches which are in Asia; unto Ephesus, (your Church) and unto Smyrna, and unto Pergamos, and unto Thyatira, and unto Sardis, and unto Philadelphia, and unto Laodicea." (These were the 7 churches discussed in Revelation, the churches that fell under John's direct influence at this time.)

Essentially what God said was, "I'm about to show you something John, and I want you to take notes!" Revelation 1:12, "And I turned to see the voice that spake with me. And being turned, I saw seven golden candlesticks." We do not have to speculate what these candlesticks are, they are explained in verse 20. "The mystery of the seven stars which thou sawest in My right hand, and the seven golden candlesticks. The seven stars are the angels of the seven churches: and the seven candlesticks which thou sawest are the seven churches." So, the seven golden candlesticks are the seven churches that Jesus just told John to write to. The church is supposed to be a light shining out into a dark world, not a candle hidden under a bed. Matthew 5: 14-16, "(14) Ye are the light of the world. A city that is set on an hill cannot be hid. (15) Neither do men light a candle, and put it under a bushel, but on a candlestick; and it giveth light unto all that are in the house. (16) Let your light so shine before men, that they may see your good works, and glorify your Father which is in heaven."

The word translated as "angel" means "messenger." It would be nice to think that every church has an angel watching over it and that may very well be the case, but I don't think you would have to write a letter to an angel to let him know what is going on. That being the case, who is the messenger that is referred to here? It is the leader of those churches, or the pastor. So, John is making notes that he will send to the pastors of these seven churches.

Revelation 1:13, "In the midst of the seven candlesticks one like unto the Son of Man, clothed with a garment down to the foot, and girt about the paps with a golden girdle." Biblically, we were first introduced to the Son of Man in Daniel 7:13-14; "I saw in the night visions, and, behold, one like the Son of Man came with the clouds of heaven, and came to the Ancient of days, and they brought Him near before Him. And there was given Him dominion, and glory, and a kingdom, that all people, nations, and languages, should serve Him: His dominion is an everlasting dominion, which shall not pass away, and His kingdom that which shall not be destroyed."

It was in Matthew 26:2 that Jesus identified Himself to His Disciples by saying; "Ye know that after two days is the feast of the Passover, and the Son of Man is betrayed to be crucified." They seemed to accept that without any question. But, in Matthew 26:63-65, it's a different story. "And the

High Priest answered and said unto Him, I adjure thee by the living God, that thou tell us whether thou be the Christ, the Son of God. Jesus saith unto him, thou hast said: nevertheless, I say unto you, hereafter shall ye see the Son of Man sitting on the right hand of power and coming in the clouds of heaven. Then the high priest rent his clothes, saying, He hath spoken blasphemy; what further need have we of witnesses? behold, now ye have heard His blasphemy." They understood what Jesus meant when He referred to Himself as the Son of Man, but rather than accept Him as their Messiah, they chose instead to put Him to death. The authority of the One speaking to John is being plainly declared in terms that are verified throughout Scripture. He who is, He who was, and He who is to come.

John spent more than three years with Jesus during His earthly ministry. He caught a brief glimpse of the glory of the Lord on the Mount of Transfiguration, but John had never seen the Lord like he is seeing Him now. Revelation 1:13-16, "And in the midst of the seven candlesticks one like unto the Son of man, clothed with a garment down to the foot, and girt about the paps with a golden girdle. His head and His hairs were white like wool, as white as snow; and His eyes were as a flame of fire; And His feet like unto fine brass, as if they burned in a furnace; and His voice as the sound of many waters."

Was this the first time someone had seen Jesus like this? Daniel 10:4-6 says "And in the four and twentieth day of the first month, as I was by the side of the great river, which is Hiddekel; then I lifted up mine eyes, and looked, and behold a certain Man clothed in linen, whose loins were girded with fine gold of Uphaz: His body also was like the beryl, and His face as the appearance of lightning, and His eyes as lamps of fire, and His arms and His feet like in color to polished brass, and the voice of His words like the voice of a multitude." Clearly, Daniel and John are seeing the same Man.

Revelation 1:17, "And when I saw Him, I fell at His feet as dead. And He laid His right hand upon me, saying unto me, Fear not; I am the first and the last." Simply stated, John passed out when He saw the glory of the Lord.

What about Daniel? Daniel 10:8-11, "Therefore I was left alone, and saw this great vision, and there remained no strength in me: for my comeliness was turned in me into corruption, and I retained no strength. Yet heard I the voice of His words: and when I heard the voice of His words, then was I in a deep sleep on my face, and my face toward the ground. And, behold, a hand touched me, which set me upon my knees and upon the palms of my hands. And He said unto me, O Daniel, a man greatly beloved, understand the words that I speak unto thee, and stand upright: for unto thee am I now sent. And when He had spoken this word unto me, I stood trembling." It is an awesome and humbling thing when we are drawn into the presence of a holy God.

Remember, that John the beloved Disciple, the one who had put his head on the chest of Jesus at the last supper, had been around and seen Jesus numerous times for a little over three years during His earthly ministry. In 1 John 1:1; John said, "that which we have heard, which we have seen with our eyes, which we have looked upon, and our hands have handled, of the Word of life." John is saying in this verse, that he saw Him, he heard Him, and he even touched Him. But what John saw during those 3 years does not compare to this. Daniel saw the pre-incarnate Christ in His glory and now John in the book of Revelation sees the resurrected Christ in all His glory, and neither of them could stand in His presence.

For years, I've listened to self-professed super saints who boast of being in the presence of God, and they strut around like it's no big deal. But those that I read about in the Bible who truly found themselves in the presence of the One True Living God, fell on their face in awe and began to humbly worship Him. God deliver us from the self-aggrandizing attitude that infects too many in this 21st century.

III
The Seven Churches

As we move into chapter 2 of the Revelation, we see the beginning of the letters to the seven churches. People try to take these seven churches and break them down into seven different church ages. That is not a Biblical concept. It is a man-made teaching. These seven churches actually existed when John wrote each of them a letter nearly two thousand years ago, and you see examples of each of these seven churches today. Nowhere in Scripture are they used to define a specific point in time as is often taught.

I believe a more accurate understanding of these churches is that they show a progression of what can happen to any church at any point in time. Churches begin deeply devoted to Christ as we see in the second chapter of Acts. But with the passing of time, some leave their first love. As their love for Christ begins to wane, they seek more of the pleasures and riches of this world. Sometimes, in order to accomplish that, churches water down their convictions and open the door for false doctrine, all under the banner of "inclusion". They come to a place where they still consider themselves a church, but they have completely rejected the authority of the Word of God. It ultimately reaches a place to where it makes God sick. And after a while, He will spew them out of His mouth while they continue to play church.

This scenario is playing itself out in front of our eyes today. Ephesus, who left its first love, as well as Pergamos and Thyatira with their false doctrine, are every much as indicative of the day we live in as is Laodicea. As best I can tell, this idea of seven different church ages became popular with John Nelson Darby in the 1800's and was soon picked up by others until now most people accept it as a Bible truth. In reality, the seven different church ages were invented by man not decreed by God. There are lessons that we need to learn and warnings that we need to heed from each of these seven churches right now.

Ephesus

Revelation 2:1 begins by saying; "Unto the angel of the church of Ephesus write..." While in the strictest sense the letter is directed to the church, notice that the message is to the angel of that church. Operating under the premise that the angel or the messenger is the pastor, these words are directed to the pastors of these seven churches. Who had been the pastor of Ephesus? John had been. Of course, while John was on Patmos someone else was serving as pastor, and this letter could have been intended for him. There is a great truth, perhaps a great warning that we miss if we try to remove John from this equation.

This letter will contain commendations, good things. It will also contain condemnations, things that were not good. It will conclude with a call to action. What are you going to do? That question is still reverberating down through time. What are we going to do?

Revelation 2:1-7, "(1) Unto the angel of the church of Ephesus write; These things saith He that holdeth the seven stars in His right hand, who walketh in the midst of the seven golden candlesticks; (2) I know thy works, and thy labour, and thy patience, and how thou canst not bear them which are evil: and thou hast tried them which say they are apostles, and are not, and hast found them liars: (3) And hast borne, and hast patience, and for My name's sake hast labored, and hast not fainted. (4) Nevertheless, I have somewhat against thee, because thou hast left thy first love. (5) Remember therefore from whence thou art fallen, and repent, and do the first works; or else I will come unto thee quickly, and will remove thy candlestick out of his place, except thou repent. (6) But this thou hast, that thou hatest the deeds of the Nicolaitans, which I also hate. (7) He that hath an ear, let him hear what the Spirit saith unto the churches; To him that overcometh will I give to eat of the tree of life which is in the midst of the paradise of God."

Jesus is saying, "These are My words to the pastors that I am holding in my right hand and to the churches that I walk in the midst of. Can you close your eyes and imagine what an incredible sight this is? The message to the church at Ephesus was:

#1. "I know your works." I have been watching you; I know what you have been doing." Ephesians 2:8 tells us that we are saved by grace through faith, but James 2:20 reminds us we live out our faith with good works. "Faith without works is dead." (James 2:20) So, the members of the church in Ephesus are putting their faith into action, and the Lord is proud of them for doing that.

#2. "your labor." In other words, it's not always easy to do good things, especially when you are surrounded by a wicked culture. But, you press on in spite of difficult circumstances.

#3. "your patience." You have not given up. Year after year you continue to do good works, even when it's not easy to do. I commend you for that.

#4. "you cannot tolerate those who are evil and wicked." You not only have Godly standards, but you are not afraid to confront wickedness.

#5. "you have tested those who say they are Apostles and found them to be liars." False prophets have always been a problem. There were phony prophets in the first century, and there are phony prophets in the twenty-first century. People who consider themselves Christians but do not read and study the Bible become easy victims to the lies of the devil. We are living in a day when rather than stoning false prophets, we make celebrities of them and make them rich by purchasing their false prophecies. God have mercy on us.

#6. "you have persevered and endured hardship for My name." Throughout history, there have been times when people suffered greatly for no other reason than the fact that they were Christians. For the most part, we have not had to experience that in America until recently. Today, there is an effort to push God out of every corner of our culture, and the devil is running rampant to destroy everything we love and cherish. It is not difficult to foresee a day in the not so distant future when Americans will suffer great persecution for no other reason than the fact that they are Christians. That would have been unthinkable a few years ago, but unless America has a real revival, it almost certainly will happen.

#7. "you have not fainted, or you have not grown weary." In spite of everything you've faced, you have not quit.

Having said these things, the message followed, "Nevertheless, I have somewhat against thee because thou hast left thy first love." Notice that wording. It does not say they had lost their first love, which is how it is often misquoted, it says they left their first love. There is an enormous difference between losing something and leaving something. If

I lost something, I probably don't know where I lost it. But if I leave something, it is a deliberate act that I am fully conscious of.

Remember that John had served as the pastor of the church in Ephesus. Is this letter being written to the person who is currently serving as pastor while John is exiled on Patmos, or is the Lord dealing with something that happened during John's tenure as pastor at Ephesus?

Have you ever asked yourself why anyone would want to be a pastor? While there are many rewarding days, there are also some exceedingly difficult days. There will always be people who do not like you. There are always unrealistic expectations, some that come from the membership and some that are self-imposed. Why would anyone want to be a pastor? The simple explanation is this; we were so in love with Jesus when we felt called into the ministry that we were willing to do whatever He wanted us to do. We loved Jesus with all our hearts and were willing to follow His call, wherever that might lead.

But, if we are not careful, we can reach a point where we become so busy with the vocation of ministry that we become guilty of just going through religious motions. If John was in truth not just the pastor of Ephesus but the spiritual advisor or administrator of the other six churches, his time could have become so consumed with all the good things that he was doing that he no longer had time for what was the most important. Let me hasten to add that this can happen to anyone, not just pastors. We must guard our hearts and fan the flame of our love for Christ.

Revelation 2:6, "But this thou hast, that thou hatest the deeds of the Nicolaitans, which I also hate." The Nicolaitans were that group within the church who always promoted compromise. God told Moses in Exodus 19:6, "And ye shall be unto Me a kingdom of priests, and a holy nation." Priests speak to God on behalf of the people and to the people on behalf of God. We are supposed to be a unique people, a called-out people. 2 Corinthians 6:17, "Wherefore come out from among them, and be ye separate, saith the Lord, and touch not the unclean thing; and I will receive you." We are in the world, but we are not like the world. Our job is to hold up the mirror of the reality of God's Word so the world can see God. Our calling is to take the Gospel to those sinking in sin and bring them to the lifeboat. This world is coming to an end, and we see that in vivid description on the pages of the book of Revelation. Our calling is to help reach as many as possible with the Gospel.

The Nicolaitans were that group within the church who said it was acceptable to adopt the culture of the world so we can "fit in". The idea is that by "fitting in", we can transform the world. The sad thing is that never works. We never win the world by becoming like the world.

Verse 7, "He that hath an ear, let him hear what the Spirit saith unto the churches; To him that overcometh will I give to eat of the tree of life, which is in the midst of the paradise of God." Here Jesus is basically saying, "Take My commendations, and take heed to My corrections or else I will remove the candlestick from its place." Ephesus, the key church in this revelation that Jesus was giving to John was in danger of destruction if they failed to repent. I pray that none of us will ever leave our first love. Let us dig a little deeper into the church at Ephesus. Located near the mouth of the Cayster River, Ephesus was one of the most easily accessible cities in Asia, both by land and sea. Its port on the Aegean Sea was one of the greatest in the ancient world. Three major roads led from Ephesus. One went east towards Babylon via Laodicea, another to the north via Smyrna, and a third went south through the Meander Valley.

A letter was written in the second century by Ignatius, one of the early church fathers who had been arrested and was being taken to Rome where he would be martyred. As he passed through Ephesus, Ignatius called it, "the highway of martyrs" because of the many Christians who had been arrested in that region and sent to Rome to be put to death.

Ephesus was the center of worship to the goddess Diana, one of the chief deities of the ancient world. The Temple in Ephesus built to honor her was one of the seven wonders in the ancient world. The image of Diana was one of the most sacred images in that day. This meant that Ephesus had a very lucrative economy because of this intense pagan worship. People came from all over the world to buy amulets and trinkets with supposed magical power. It is important to understand this because in Acts chapter 19, when the Apostle Paul is in Ephesus, you see that the city has this obsession with pagan spiritualism.

There was also a great deal of sexual immorality that was associated with the cult of the goddess Diana. Known as sacred prostitution, immorality in the guise of worshipping this goddess was a common part of life in Ephesus.

The city of Ephesus had a lot of evil going on within the temple of Diana, the pagan worship, the sexual immorality, and sorcery. The church at Ephesus also had to deal with people who claimed to be apostles but were not. They tested them and found them to be liars and false prophets. Then, there was this group called the Nicolaitans. This was a group of people with a so-called special revelation that essentially allowed them to be able to participate in any type of behavior that they wanted in terms of morality and the flesh as long as they professed God and Christ in their minds.

If you go back to Acts chapters 19 and 20, you will find a lot of details of the events that took place there, even down to Paul's farewell address to the elders of the church. We have a letter addressed to the church called the book of Ephesians. We also have two letters called First and Second Timothy. Timothy served as one of the pastors of Ephesus. So, we have the books of Ephesians and Timothy along with references in the book of Acts that deal with some of the issues impacting the church in Ephesus during that time. That is quite a bit of Bible information on this one church. If a city ever needed a church, Ephesus did.

When the Apostle Paul came to Ephesus, he found disciples whose knowledge was limited to the baptism of John. Paul laid his hands upon them, and they received the Holy Ghost. We know from Acts:19, that miracles were part of Paul's ministry in Ephesus. People were healed and demons were cast out. The stark contrast between the Gospel of Jesus Christ and the sorcery and black arts within Ephesus led to confrontations due to the great response to Paul's preaching of the Gospel.

Acts 19:17-19, "(17) And this was known to all the Jews and Greeks also dwelling at Ephesus; and fear fell on them all, and the name of the Lord Jesus was magnified. (18) And many that believed came, and confessed, and shewed their deeds. (19) Many of them also which used curious arts brought their books together and burned them before all men: and they counted the price of them and found it fifty thousand pieces of silver."

The response to the Gospel was so great that when we look at verses 23-27, we see that the income of Demetrius and other silversmiths who crafted images of Diana was significantly affected. You've heard the expression, "follow the money." If you want to understand certain things, follow the money. If you follow the money in this story, you realize that the ministry of Paul was getting into the pocketbooks of these silversmiths.

In Revelation 2:5, Jesus tells the church at Ephesus to repent and do their first works. What were their first works? They are recorded in Acts:19 as a great response to the Gospel, people coming into the church, the renouncing of immorality and paganism, abandoning of the cult of Diana, burning their books of witchcraft, and turning from a life of darkness to the light of the knowledge of Jesus Christ.

In Acts 20, Paul is making his way back to Jerusalem when he stops at Miletus and sends word for the elders of the church at Ephesus to come see him. It is a very moving passage where Paul tells them that they are not going to see him anymore. Then he gives them this warning: "(29) For I know this, that after my departing shall grievous wolves enter in among you, not sparing the flock. (30) Also, of your own selves shall men arise, speaking perverse things, to draw away disciples after them."

In Revelation, chapter 2, what Paul predicted had sadly come to pass, but the church withstood them. Have you ever wondered how different the church would be if more pastors and elders stood against the false prophets of our day and said, "You are a liar"? There are wolves in sheep's clothing today who have the same motive that the false prophets at Ephesus had. The motive is to draw people to themselves, and away from the church. Unscrupulous, so-called "ministers" prey on the emotions and fears of people who are not well versed in the Scriptures. All you have to do is "follow the money" to see that this is the case. Christ commended the church at Ephesus for their stance against false doctrine.

The church of the twenty-first century has in many ways become like the church of the first century at Ephesus. The failure to stand against false doctrine from within the church leaves the church powerless to confront the evil outside the church. We must get back to the Bible, and what "thus saith the Lord."

Ephesians 2:1-6 "(1) And you hath He quickened, who were dead in trespasses and sins; (2) Wherein in time past ye walked according to the course of this world, according to the prince of the power of the air, the spirit that now worketh in the children of disobedience: (3) Among whom also we all had our conversation in times past in the lusts of our flesh, fulfilling the desires of the flesh and of the mind; and were by nature the children of wrath, even as others. (4) But God, who is rich in mercy, for His great love wherewith He loved us, (5) Even when we were dead in sins, hath quickened us together with Christ, (by grace ye are saved;) (6) And hath raised us up together and made us sit together in heavenly places in Christ Jesus."

The members at Ephesus once walked in those ways of the world. They went to the Roman baths, pagan shrines, and places where all types of lewd behavior occurred. They had walked into the temple of Diana and engaged in sacred prostitution thinking they were worshipping the goddess and that it was okay. Ephesians 5:8, "For ye were sometimes darkness, but now are ye light in the Lord: walk as children of light."

A first love is far more than every emotional feeling you had when you first came to know the truth. Whatever it was that you felt then is not exactly the sum total and definition of first love. You can never have that emotion again, but you can do the first works again. You can rekindle a love for God and go into a deeper commitment to God at any age.

In the book of Acts, we see the new converts in Ephesus burning their books of witchcraft and abandoning idolatry, coming out of the dark dominant pagan culture of the first century and moving toward the light of the Gospel of Jesus Christ and the kingdom of God. They were totally committed to Christ. This is what the Church in Ephesus in the book of Revelation is being called to return to, and this is one of the great lessons that we learn from this first letter.

Did you know that John is the only person who uses the word "antichrist" in the entire Bible? In 1st & 2nd John, he talks about an antichrist (singular), and antichrists (plural.) Both one antichrist, but also many antichrists. He is basically saying that if you fall for false teachers in your midst now, you will fall for the great Antichrist who is yet to come. If you fall for the little antichrists, the little false prophets, you will fall for the big one. 1 John 4:1, "Beloved, believe not every spirit, but try the spirits whether they are of God: because many false prophets are gone out into the world."

Paul tells Timothy to pursue righteousness and godliness and faith and love and endurance and gentleness. 1 Timothy 1:5-6, "The purpose of the commandment is love from a pure heart, and of a good conscience, and of sincere faith. From which some having strayed have turned aside to idle talk."

"Love from a pure heart." What did Christ say about the church at Ephesus in the book of Revelation? He said they had left their first love. Timothy is admonished to teach the church at Ephesus to hold onto a pure love. As you hold onto sound doctrine and resist those who inject false teaching, you will be holding fast in the way of a pure heart.

Let's go back to Revelation 2:7. "He that hath an ear, let him hear what the Spirit saith unto the churches; To him that overcometh will I give to eat of the tree of life, which is in the midst of the paradise of God." God has something awesome planned for all those who will overcome. We will look at this tree of life later in our study.

Smyrna

What would you think of Christians who lived in poverty and who were hated by their neighbors? In the book of Revelation, the church at Smyrna is known for their poverty and persecution, yet Jesus calls them "rich."

Revelation 2:8-11, "(8) And unto the angel of the church in Smyrna write; These things saith the First and the Last, which was dead, and is alive; (9) I know thy works, and tribulation, and poverty, (but thou art rich) and I know the blasphemy of them which say they are Jews, and are not, but are the synagogue of Satan. (10) Fear none of those things which thou shalt suffer: behold, the devil shall cast some of you into prison, that ye may be tried; and ye shall have tribulation ten days: be thou faithful unto death, and I will give thee a crown of life. (11) He that hath an ear, let him hear what the Spirit saith unto the churches; He that overcometh shall not be hurt of the second death."

Smyrna is located to the north of Ephesus. There's nothing left of the ancient city now but a crumbling wall in a city park on a hill overlooking the Turkish city of İzmir. Smyrna was the home of Polycarp, an elder in the church, who was martyred in the second century because of his faith. According to Irenaeus, who knew him, Polycarp was a disciple of the Apostle John. Other church fathers confirm this, recording also that he was ordained by John as Bishop of Smyrna. When Polycarp was 86 years old, he was told to renounce Christ or he would be burned alive. He responded by saying, "I have served the Lord for many years, and He never renounced me; how then can I blaspheme my Lord and Savior and renounce Him?" There is a statue of Polycarp in Izmir today, said to be on the spot where he was burned at the stake. Polycarp's strong faith was typical of the Christians who lived in Smyrna during this time.

Just as we saw with the church at Ephesus, there are words of commendation, but unlike Ephesus, there are no words of condemnation. Does that mean they were a perfect church? No. But when you are a church where martyrdom is common and you have to make a bold stand for Christ, it does tend to eliminate some of the petty issues that days of prosperity seem to bring.

Unlike the church at Ephesus, there is not much said about Smyrna in the Bible other than these few verses. Smyrna was a very beautiful city in its time. It was a fairly large city because, like Ephesus, it had a harbor. It was known for music, known for its culture, known for theater, and it was known as a world trade center. Goods from all over the Mediterranean came through Smyrna. There was a lot of wealth in Smyrna, but not for the Christians.

Smyrna was also famous for something else. Around 195 B.C., they saw a new power rising in the Mediterranean so they declared themselves the ally of Rome. Around that same time, they built a temple to worship and sacrifice to the gods of Rome. They had one temple that was dedicated to worshipping the Roman Emperor.

Revelation 2:8, "Unto the angel of the church in Smyrna write: These things saith the first and the last, which was dead and is alive." Why did Jesus introduce Himself as the One Who was "dead and is alive"? He is smacking emperor worship right in the teeth. Emperors were so-called gods who died but did not come back to life. He proclaimed Himself to be one who had died but was resurrected to life again.

There are no words of correction to this congregation, and yet they are a church in tribulation. The Greek word that is translated poverty doesn't mean that they were just poor people. It means they were utterly destitute. We are looking at people living in the street. We are looking at people who can't feed themselves. However, it says later in the same verse, "but you are rich." Physically these people were destitute, but spiritually they were rich.

The church in Smyrna suffered great tribulation. Revelation 2:10, "Fear none of those things which thou shalt suffer: behold, the devil shall cast some of you into prison, that ye may be tried; and ye shall have tribulation ten days: be thou faithful unto death, and I will give thee a crown of life."

Their works were right before God. They were rich before God, but they were in constant tribulation. Sometimes we look at a situation such as this and say, if they were persecuted, if they went through all this tribulation and lived through all this poverty, obviously God wasn't pleased with them. Let's look at what Jesus said in the Sermon on the Mount. Matthew 5:10-12, "(10) Blessed are they which are persecuted for righteousness' sake: for theirs is the kingdom of heaven. (11) Blessed are ye, when men shall revile you, and persecute you, and shall say all manner of evil against you falsely, for My sake. (12) Rejoice and be exceeding glad: for great is your reward in heaven: for so persecuted they the prophets which were before you." A key word in verse eleven, that is not often pointed out, is the word "falsely." There is a big difference between false accusations that bring persecution and in persecution for actions that may be justly deserved.

I don't know about you, I would like a blessing, but I'm not sure I want this one. We can't look at the situation in Smyrna, and say, "Oh, there was something wrong with those people." It is just the opposite. They were special people who stayed faithful during a time when they were suffering extreme persecution. In Revelation 2:10, Jesus tells them to not fear any of those things which you are about to suffer. "Be faithful until death and I will give you the crown of life."

Revelation 2:11, "He that hath an ear, let him hear what the Spirit saith unto the churches; He that overcometh shall not be hurt of the second death." So, these people who follow the First and the Last, the One who died and was resurrected, the real Emperor, the real King, they are going to be persecuted, but they are promised eternal life for their faithfulness.

Today, we are facing an increasingly secular humanistic society. We live in a world where we could experience serious persecution for what we believe. Many places around the world already are. If and when we do encounter persecution for our faith, we must pray and stay close to God. We must remember that there were people who went before us who remained faithful, unto death. The church at Smyrna, the persecuted church, is our example.

Pergamos

The church at Pergamos is an intriguing study. We need to look at what was taking place historically in each of these seven churches and how that could come into effect during the last days. I realize some of my understanding is speculative. I don't claim to have all the answers. There are too many people through the years who thought they knew exactly what and how everything was going to take place in the end times. And they have been proven wrong time and time again. To me, an effective Bible study is one that makes people think. I will give you some historical information that may possibly play itself out later in our study. Hopefully, we can all learn as we go.

Revelation 2:12, "And to the angel of the church in Pergamos write." Pergamos is the northernmost of the seven churches. The city was actually an acropolis, which means it was built on the top of a mountain, but the mountain top was flat much like the Acropolis in Athens, Greece. However, the one in Pergamos was much larger. It even had a theatre on the hillside like the one in Greece. Pergamos was a very wealthy city. It had the second greatest library in the ancient world. The greatest, of course, was in Alexandria, Egypt.

In the first century, the city of Pergamos was the chief governmental city of all the church cities mentioned in the book of Revelation. Most of this ancient city lay at the foot of a mountain, but part of the city and the religious temples were built on top of the mountain. In 133 B.C., Attalus III, the last king of Pergamos died without an heir so he willed the city to Rome. Pergamos became the center of Roman authority in Asia Minor, and it became a place of emperor worship, even more so than at Smyrna. An ancient coin was discovered at Pergamos that shows a depiction of Augustus. In 12 A.D., Augustus declared himself to be the Pontifex Maximus, the chief priest of Rome and head of the Collegium Pontificum. He was the highest priest in the land. There is a famous statue of Augustus in the Museum of Roman History in Rome, Italy, that shows Augustus wearing the robe of the Pontifex Maximus. "Pontifex Maximus" -- have you heard of that before? There is an individual in Rome who still bears that title today. He is best known as "The Pope." Historically speaking, at some point, the office of Caesar and the office of the Pope blended into one after Christianity became the state religion. The kingdom and the authority that once belonged to Caesar became the kingdom of the Pope. It was an unusual mixture of political and religious power that occasionally had tragic side effects. In that sense, the Holy Roman Empire never ceased to exist.

There was also a temple in Pergamos dedicated to Asclepius, the serpent-god, the God of healing. The rod of Asclepius, a snake-entwined staff, remains a symbol of medicine today. Galen, one of the foremost doctors of the ancient world who is sometimes referred to as the father of medical science, lived and studied at Pergamos in this temple.

Revelation 2:12, "And to the angel of the church in Pergamos write; These things saith He which hath the sharp sword with two edges." A Roman sword was the symbol of Roman authority. Using that symbol, Jesus is establishing that He has more power and authority than the emperor and the culture of that Roman world. And. that power is His Word.

Rome perceived the Christians' allegiance to Christ as a threat to their government and consequently tried to silence them through persecution. This scenario is repeating itself today in our own beloved America. Wickedness, frightened by godliness, will always lash out at Christian values. Any threat to Roman order in the first century was met with the two-edged sword of Roman authority. The church at Pergamos understood what Jesus was saying when He said, "I have a two-edged sword, and it is sharper." Hebrews 4:12, "For the Word of God is quick, and powerful, and sharper than any two-edged sword, piercing even to the dividing asunder of soul and spirit, and of the joints and marrow, and is a discerner of the thoughts and intents of the heart."

There are some verses in the Bible that cause you to immediately pause and give serious consideration to what is being said. Revelation 2:13 is one of those verses. "I know thy works, and where thou dwellest, even where Satan's seat is and thou holdest fast My name, and hast not denied My faith, even in those days wherein Antipas was My faithful martyr, who was slain among you, where Satan dwelleth."

In spite of the evil that surrounded them and all of the man-made gods, some of the Christians at Pergamos had not denied the faith. And as we saw in Smyrna, there were people who died for their faith. This brief statement in this one verse is all we know about Antipas, but some of you may recognize the name. It is not a Jewish name. It is not a name that a Jewish person would have had in Pergamos at this time or probably at any other time. "Antipas" is the name given to a ruler that we read about in the Gospels. His name was Herod Antipas, son of Herod the great. He was a ruler of Judea. He was the one who had John the Baptist and the Apostle James put to death. In the book of Acts, chapter 12, he dies a horrendous death. No Jewish person would have taken this name. Antipas was almost certainly a gentile who became a convert to Christianity and then died a martyr's death. History is filled with untold numbers of faithful men and women who died for their faith

Jesus said to Pergamos, "I know who you are, I know where you live, and I know that Satan's seat is where you live." Satan's seat is not mentioned in any of the other six letters, but it is mentioned twice in this one verse. This is an exclusive message to this church. Satan's seat was the temple built in Pergamos to worship Zeus. In ancient mythology, Zeus ruled as king of the gods on Mount Olympus. If you ever visit Pergamos, you will not see this temple unless your journey also carries you to Germany. In the late 1800's, German archeologists excavated this area and the altar was taken stone by stone to Berlin where it was reassembled. In 1930, The Pergamum Museum in Berlin was opened to the public.

This altar in Germany, taken from Pergamos, has an eerie connection to Adolf Hitler. In the 1930's, after Hitler had taken control, he began to build what he called his Third Reich, a world order that he said would last for 1,000 years. Hitler enlisted Albert Speer as his chief architect. Speer was tasked with rebuilding Germany, the monuments, the stadiums, and all the government buildings. When you see the black and white news reels from the 1930's of the Nazis having their political rallies in Nuremburg, you see a complex that was designed by Speer called the "Zeppelin Field." If you look at the façade, you will see that Speer modeled this building after the altar of Zeus from Pergamos. Speer's structure is on a much grander scale, but the design was taken from the altar to the chief god, Zeus, who was worshipped in the place where Jesus said Satan dwells.

Inside the German rally grounds, thousands of Nazi Party members marched in torchlight parades. From the altar's podium, Hitler mesmerized the crowds as they swore a "holy oath" to Germany. From 1933 to 1938 hundreds of thousands of Germans gathered at the Zeppelin Field, but the 1934 rally captured the attention of the world because of the propaganda film, "Triumph of the Will." It was a documentary about Hitler and the Nazi Party. In the film, Hitler was portrayed as a messiah who descends through the clouds to the faithful waiting for him below.

In 2006, in the *Archeology Today Magazine*, an article was written entitled, "Revelations from Revelation, Satan's throne." Satan wants to be worshipped; he always has. At some point in the future, a leader will arise who seems to have all the answers for the ills of this world. And just as we have seen from history, multitudes will follow him to the point that they worship him as God.

Keep in mind that the Roman Empire during this time was the fourth part of the image that King Nebuchadnezzar saw in the book of Daniel chapter 7. (Babylon, Persia, Greece, and Rome) Later in our study, we will see how these nations mentioned in the book of Daniel have unfolded over the course of history. And some will still have an impact on the events of the last days.

Unlike Smyrna however, there is some condemnation to the church in Pergamos. Revelation 2:14, "But I have a few things against thee, because thou hast there them that hold the doctrine of Balaam, who taught Balac to cast a stumblingblock before the children of Israel, to eat things sacrificed unto idols, and to commit fornication."

Remember the story in Numbers, chapter 22, where a donkey speaks? Balaam was hired to curse the children of Israel and God told him that he couldn't do it. So, Balaam did what far too many people have done when they desire to please man more than God, and especially when men are offering to pay you. He came up with a compromise. Let me hasten to say that it was Balaam's compromise, not God's.

According to 2 Peter 2:15, Balaam "loved the wages of unrighteousness" more than he loved obeying God. He basically sold his soul for wealth and popularity with man. Balaam knew what pleased the Lord but what pleased the Lord did not please Balaam. Balaam told Balac to just become friends with these people, just assimilate with them, marry their sons and daughters. That way, they would become one people. Once they adopt your ways, they will no longer be a threat to you. Instead of leading the children of Israel away from idolatry and sexual immorality, Balaam led them to it. That sounds like the church of the twenty-first century. We have brought so much of the world into the church that the world no longer feels exposed by the church. Rather than the world accepting God, we have accepted the gods of this world.

Revelation 2:15 says, "So hast thou also them that hold the doctrine of the Nicolaitans, which thing I hate." If you remember from our study on the church at Ephesus, the Nicolaitans were that group within the church who said it's okay to adopt the culture of the world so we can fit in. And by fitting in, we can transform the world. The sad thing is that it never works. God is not pleased when people do that. The doctrine of Balaam and the Nicolaitans conforms to the culture of the world rather than seeking to transform the world by the power of God's Word. In strong language, Jesus says, "I hate their teachings". Because it is a false teaching, He tells them to repent.

Between those who hold the doctrine of Balaam for the sake of personal gain at the expense of displeasing God and those who follow the teaching of the Nicolaitans which Jesus hates, we have a group of people who have decided that compromise with the surrounding culture is the best way to go. If we put the pieces together that have been given to us in the first two chapters of Revelation, this is what we see. The church at Pergamos has a candlestick, and Christ is in the midst of that candlestick as the head of the church. But then, you have two groups of people within the church, some who are faithful in their relationship with Christ and some who have decided to compromise with the world system. There are some who were willing to die for their faith, but some who held to the doctrine of Balaam and the Nicolaitans which Jesus hates.

God says to the church at Pergamos in verses 16 and 17, "Repent; or else I will come unto thee quickly and will fight against them with the sword of My mouth. He that hath an ear, let him hear what the Spirit saith unto the churches; To him that overcometh will I give to eat of the hidden manna, and will give him a white stone, and in the stone a new name written, which no man knoweth saving he that receiveth it." Simply stated, God said He would bring judgment on all who continued to live this way. But then on the positive side, God said that to those who overcome, He would give to eat of the hidden manna, and He would give them a white stone that has a new name written on it.

The hidden manna is an obvious reference to Christ, the Bread of Life. But then, Jesus says, "I will give him a white stone, and on the stone a new name written which no one knows except he who receives it." A new name; a white stone.

In ancient Greece, jury members would cast a white stone to signify an acquittal. To receive a white stone meant that you were free from condemnation. You had been tried and had been found worthy.

In the Roman world, there was a small object called a "tessera." It was made of stone or clay or bone and conveyed special privileges to its owner. The ancient Romans used "tesserae" as tokens of admittance to various kinds of events. Perhaps the best thought regarding the meaning of the white stone has to do with the ancient Roman custom of awarding white stones to the victors of athletic games. The winner of a contest was awarded a white stone with his name inscribed on it. This served as his "ticket" to a special awards banquet. If we look at it from this possibility, Jesus is promising the overcomers entrance to the eternal victory celebration in heaven and the greatest banquet the world has ever seen, the Marriage Supper of the Lamb.

The entry ticket is a white stone with a new name. To a member of the church at Pergamos 2,000 years ago, this was another instance that they could easily relate to. Augustus was the first of the Roman Caesars, but that was not his original name. His original name was Octavian. He was the great nephew of Julius Caesar. After Julius Caesar's death and after Octavian defeated Mark Anthony, he took on the name Augustus. Augustus was a name used within the Roman world to only speak about the gods. No human had ever held that name before, but Octavian changed his name to

Augustus and was worshipped as a god. Jesus said to the church at Pergamus, "I am going to give you a new name." Because there was a temple dedicated to the worship of Augustus in Pergamos, they understood exactly what Jesus was saying. Christians who overcame the world and who did not bow a knee to Satan would be given entrance into a kingdom above all other kingdoms, the kingdom of our God.

What do we learn from the church at Pergamos? We learn that Satan continues to exert a relentless pressure in our world today from the temptation to compromise, to watering down our faith, to fudging our convictions for convenience sake. We end up going along so we can get along. But God is looking for those who will contend for the faith and will avoid compromising with the evil of this world. The letter to the church at Pergamos is a piece of living history because the message to that church certainly applies to Christians today as we contend with a world that, in many ways, is just like the world of Pergamos in the first century. In our modern world, the temptations take on different forms, but the struggles are just as real. I hope we can learn from Pergamos, and be encouraged to be faithful, even as Antipas was.

Thyatira

The fourth church in Revelation is Thyatira. This church is a little southeast of Pergamos. Do we know anyone from Thyatira? Yes, we do. Acts 16:14, "And a certain woman named Lydia, a seller of purple, of the city of Thyatira, which worshipped God, heard us: whose heart the Lord opened, that she attended unto the things which were spoken of Paul." Thyatira was the hometown of Lydia.

Revelation 2:18-22, "(18) And unto the angel of the church in Thyatira write; These things saith the Son of God, who hath His eyes like unto a flame of fire, and His feet are like fine brass; (19) I know thy works, and charity, and service, and faith, and thy patience, and thy works; and the last to be more than the first. (20) Notwithstanding I have a few things against thee, because thou sufferest that woman Jezebel, which calleth herself a prophetess, to teach and to seduce My servants to commit fornication, and to eat things sacrificed unto idols. (21) And I gave her space to repent of her fornication; and she repented not. (22) Behold, I will cast her into a bed, and them that commit adultery with her into great tribulation, except they repent of their deeds."

If you look only at verse 19, you would think that Thyatira is a pretty good church. They are faithful, and they are charitable. They are patient, and their good works have steadily increased since

43

they began. But then comes verse 20. For many people today, tolerance is the only real virtue, and intolerance is seen as a vice. Of course, I have noticed that the most intolerant people in the world are the ones who can't tolerate any opinion other than their own. The message to Thyatira goes against the grain of our modern culture, and it also goes against the grain of many in the church. What we see here is that there are Godly boundaries to tolerance. The main criticism of the church at Thyatira is that it has tolerated something and someone that should not be tolerated. Tolerance can sometimes be an intolerable thing.

When you allow someone to have a platform in your church to preach or to teach doctrine that is contrary to the Word of God, it not only will be accepted by some, it will continue to spread. And over time, it will be accepted as Scriptural. Those who accept the false teaching will then begin to harshly criticize those who disagree with them as being intolerant. And if you say anything, you are quickly told that no one can judge them but God. People seem to conveniently forget that one day God will judge them, not by the standards of their culture but by the standard of His Holy Word. The spirit of Jezebel is alive and well in the modern church.

Thyatira was located along a major highway and was a commercial center. There were leather workers, linen workers, tanners, potters, bakers and other professions in Thyatira. All these groups of people came together for the benefit of their trades in something like an ancient labor union.

Since the Bible mentions this place that had become famous for its purple cloth, let's look briefly at it. Most researcher believe the purple dye was produced from the mucus of various species of marine mollusks (sea snails) that were plentiful in the Mediterranean Sea. When the German chemist, Paul Friedlander, tried to recreate Tyrian purple in 2008, he needed twelve thousand mollusks to create 1.4 ounces of dye. It was just enough to color a handkerchief and cost almost 2,000 Euros. No wonder this purple cloth was so expensive. Some people suggest that perhaps they were able to produce this purple dye from the root of a plant, but it seems most likely that it was produced from these mollusks. Purple garments could only be afforded by the very rich or by royalty.

Remember, Jesus was speaking to a literal church that existed 2,000 years ago. He was addressing issues which they faced on a daily basis. Some of the terminology that may seem a little unusual to us made perfect sense to them. We just need to understand what it was like back then so we can make a true interpretation today.

Revelation 2:18 says, "And unto the angel of the church in Thyatira write; These things saith the Son of God, who hath His eyes like unto a flame of fire, and His feet are like fine brass." This letter begins with something that isn't found anywhere else in the book of Revelation; Jesus is referred to as the "Son of God". The patron saint of the city of Thyatira was Apollo, the sun god. Standing in stark contrast to the pagan sun god, we find this description of an all-powerful Christ who has eyes of flame that will pierce right into the very heart of people and circumstances. This "Son of God" knows our motives. He can penetrate through our exterior to the core of our thoughts. He is the true "Son" of God. Hebrews 4:12, "For the Word of God is quick, and powerful, and sharper than any two-edged sword, piercing even to the dividing asunder of soul and spirit, and of the joints and marrow, and is a discerner of the thoughts and intents of the heart." It is that penetrating gaze of God that will reveal what is happening behind the scenes.

The letter to Thyatira begins with some of the best compliments given to any of the seven churches of Revelation. Jesus said, "I know your works, and love, and service, and faith, and patience", and then He tells them that their last works are greater than their first. Literally meaning, you are doing better now than you were before. If you remember, that could not be said about the church at Ephesus. Jesus told them that they needed to return to their first love because they had left it. At first glance, you are tempted to say that the church in Thyatira is a flourishing church, but when you look more closely, you see that something is terribly wrong. Revelation 2:20, "Notwithstanding I have a few things against thee, because thou sufferest that woman Jezebel, which calleth herself a prophetess, to teach and to seduce My servants to commit fornication, and to eat things sacrificed unto idols." Jesus said they were permitting and allowing certain things to happen within the church that should not be happening.

In ancient Greece, the Sybil or Oracle of Delphi, was famous for her prophesying. There was said to be such a person in Thyatira referred to as "that woman Jezebel". But, how could a pagan, who had gained the reputation of a prophetess, have the power to infiltrate the church to this level of seduction and thereby influence the whole church? What does this personification of evil do? She encourages everyone to seriously compromise their beliefs, "teaching seduction, committing sexual immorality, eating things sacrificed to idols." This lifestyle was typical among the trade guilds that I mentioned previously. And, guess what? It was important to be a participating member of the group because if you weren't, how were you going to make your living? How were you going to take care of your family? That was part of the pressure being put on the church in Thyatira. It was a poisonous doctrine that led to unbelievable sin.

Jesus continues to make the connection to Jezebel and Thyatira when He says, "I gave her time to repent of her sexual immorality." Was Jezebel of ancient times given the opportunity to repent? Yes, but ultimately, she did not repent. The church with the Jezebel spirit is also given an opportunity to repent. Verse 22; "Behold, I will cast her into a bed, and them that commit adultery with her into great tribulation, except they repent of their deeds."

Revelation 2:24-26, "(24) But unto you I say, and unto the rest in Thyatira, as many as have not this doctrine, and which have not known the depths of Satan, as they speak; I will put upon you none other burden. (25) But that which ye have already, hold fast till I come (26) And he that overcometh, and keepeth My works unto the end, to him will I give power over the nations." As in the previous churches, there were some in Thyatira who remained faithful. They had not fallen into this terrible heresy, into the "depths of Satan." To them Jesus says, hold fast, hold fast to righteousness, hold fast to what is good.

What will the end result be if you hold fast to what is true, and right and holy? Revelation 2:28-29, "(28) And I will give Him the Morning Star. (29) He that hath an ear, let him hear what the Spirit saith unto the churches." This Scripture is not saying that you will be able to get up early in the morning and see the stars. It's talking about "The Morning Star", Christ Himself. We will be given Christ. That is the greatest gift and promise of all, to be His, to be a member of God's family.

This letter to Thyatira concludes with a charge to overcome, to persevere, to keep doing what is right. In this particular letter, can we find any lessons that speak to us today? There are many. This corruption came from within the church. It was allowed by the church. We make choices every day as to how we will respond to pressures around us, pressures that seek to make us conform or to fit in with the ways of the world. Increasingly, we are told that it doesn't really matter what you believe as long as you are a nice person? That is pure heresy. Are there lifestyles that are wrong, that are unacceptable? God says there are. There are lifestyle choices that we cannot allow or condone because God doesn't allow it. To say anything else is to be a Thyatiran, and God says that is not what you want to be. From a distance, they appeared to be nice people because they had good jobs and they were able to be charitable. But it was all a religious façade. Thyatira teaches us that we cannot mix the truth of God with the ways of this world. It is unacceptable.

This letter is telling us to be careful what we tolerate. Does our commitment to Christ come first? Hold fast, keep overcoming, keep striving, keep doing God's work. There is an old song that comes to mind that says in part, "It's worth it all to be His child, to serve Him through, the last long mile..." We can be children of a holy God with all the wonderful blessings that it brings. So, let's hold fast.

Sardis

As we continue our travels southward, we come to the fifth church, the church in Sardis. This letter contains a soul-searching message. Revelation 3:1-6, "(1) And unto the angel of the church in Sardis write; These things saith He that hath the seven Spirits of God, and the seven stars; I know thy works, that thou hast a name that thou livest, and art dead. (2) Be watchful, and strengthen the things which remain, that are ready to die: for I have not found thy works perfect before God. (3) Remember therefore how thou hast received and heard, and hold fast, and repent. If therefore thou shalt not watch, I will come on thee as a thief, and thou shalt not know what hour I will come upon thee. (4) Thou hast a few names even in Sardis which have not defiled their garments; and they shall walk with Me in white: for they are worthy. (5) He that overcometh, the same shall be clothed in white raiment; and I will not blot out his name out of the book of life, but I will confess his name before My Father, and before His angels. (6) He that hath an ear, let him hear what the Spirit saith unto the churches."

Church tradition says that this area was the first to be converted by the preaching of the Apostle John. There were numerous other churches in the area, most notably Colossae which was very close to the church at Laodicea. But only seven of these area churches received letters. Sardis was one of the oldest cities in the region and was at one time the wealthy capital of the ancient kingdom of Lydia. The city was supplied with water from the Pactolus River, which also helped make the city prosperous when gold was discovered near its banks. The original city of Sardis was built on a cliff, but as it continued to grow, another city formed at the base of the cliff. They were both Sardis, but in some ways, they were like two cities separated by a cliff.

When John wrote this letter, Sardis was about 750 years old. It existed at the time of Cyrus the Great. Sardis had been famous for generations as an economic powerhouse, but by the end of the first century, it had changed dramatically and was in decline. This is important to understand because the church at Sardis reflected the decline that was going on in that city.

Jesus immediately confronts the problem facing them in verse 1, "you have a name that you are alive, but you are dead." It appears that a majority of the people in the church were spiritually dead, even though they had a reputation of being alive. When people talked about the church at Sardis, they probably said, "Have you ever gone to Sardis? Now there is a dynamic church." But Jesus says, "You are dead." There is a stark contrast between how the people of Sardis saw themselves and how

Jesus saw them. The Bible doesn't say that the church at Sardis was persecuted as the church at Smyrna was. It doesn't say that they had the false teachings of Jezebel like in Thyatira. Their problem was that they had a reputation of being alive, but they were dead.

Jesus said there were several things they needed to do. They needed to repent. They needed to strengthen what remained. They needed to remember what they had once heard and received and had obeyed. The people at Sardis had been taught the truth, but they were not living it. Jesus warned them to wake up and repent.

Revelation 3:2, "Be watchful, and strengthen the things that remain, that are ready to die." This church believes it is alive, but it is not. But praise God, there were some in Sardis who had not defiled their garments. There was a minority of members who remained committed Christians. They were faithful and Jesus said that they will walk with Him in white for they are worthy. Their names will not be blotted out of the book of life, and the Lord will acknowledge them before the Father. Inside this congregation are some who are still dedicated to God. But the implication is that the rest of them are not. This church is in serious trouble.

Notice what Jesus said in verse 5, "He that overcometh, the same shall be clothed in white raiment; and I will not blot out his name out of the book of life." This is one of the strongest condemnations given to any of the churches.

How does a church die? I'm sure there was a time when the church at Sardis didn't want to die. I'm sure at one time it was a vibrant church, an exciting place to be with people who loved and followed God. But just like the city around them, although they still maintained a good reputation, they were dying. And even more tragic, the members of the church didn't seem to realize it. If they did, they apparently didn't care.

What are some of the symptoms of a dying church? In the case of Sardis, they were not spiritually watchful. The first thing Jesus said in Revelation 3:2 was, "Be watchful..." Let's go to Luke 12:36-38, "(36) And ye yourselves like unto men that wait for their lord, when He will return from the wedding; that when He cometh and knocketh, they may open unto Him immediately. (37) Blessed are those servants, whom the Lord when He cometh shall find watching: verily I say unto you, that He shall gird himself, and make them to sit down to meat, and will come forth and serve them. (38) And if He shall come in the second watch, or come in the third watch, and find them so, blessed are those servants."

In this parable in Luke, Jesus says that to be prepared, we must be watching. If we are walking with God, we will be watching for Christ's return. If we are not walking with God, our attention will be preoccupied with everything around us, and we will begin to take our eyes off of God. If we are watching, it doesn't matter when Jesus comes because we are ready. The church at Sardis had no desire to be ready.

The problem in a dying church is that they begin to overlook the culture around them. I'm not saying that these people would have promoted sin, but they would have accepted it. They would not have promoted idolatry, but they wouldn't stand against it either. They had a reputation that they were alive, but they were not, and over time, they simply begin to decay. They got together and heard the same sermons, they said the same things to each other, and when they said good bye and headed home, they lived the same way they always had. They were religious, but spiritually lost.

What does a person do if they find themselves in such a condition? Romans 13:11-12, "(11) And that, knowing the time, that now it is high time to awake out of sleep: for now is our salvation nearer than when we believed. (12) The night is far spent, the day is at hand: let us therefore cast off the works of darkness, and let us put on the armour of light." Paul said to wake up. Remember when your heart was on fire to learn and know God's truth.

Going to church can become a social event. Being sociable is not a bad thing, but in a dying church, that is the primary reason people go to church. It becomes almost like a habit, something they have always done. The message to Sardis is important for us today because any church can die for these same reasons. There is no more watching. There is no more strengthening what we have. People in a dying church really like each other, and that becomes the main reason they go to church.

As this condition at Sardis progressed, they lost more and more of what they once had until Jesus said, "just take what you have left and let's work on that." We can reach a point that we forget how God has worked in our lives in the past. The Bible warns us in Amos 6:1, "Woe to them that are at ease in Zion."

With dying churches, it becomes almost impossible to become relevant to people outside their little group. I guess what I'm trying to say is this, "One of the major problems with a dying church is that they become comfortable with their decay."

What are the symptoms of dying churches? Most of their money and discussions focus on how to fix the building, but they have no evangelistic outreach to the lost community around them. Dying churches usually go from one extreme to the other. One is, "We have always done it this way and we have no intention of changing." The other is, "We've got to change everything." Either way, you usually end up with a church that centers itself around one particular generation. A few years ago, I heard a pastor say that no one over 45 years of age was welcome at his church. By now, that pastor is over 45 himself, but I see he hasn't left.

God's church is not a one generation church. It is a church that is founded on building the entire family of God. Can anyone tell me which age is more important in a family, or which age is not important in a family? God wants churches that are centered around Him in which everyone is involved. So, you minister to different people, of different ages, who come from different backgrounds, but there is one center, and that center is God.

Dying churches need to strengthen what they have, but they have to strengthen what is Biblically correct. Hebrews 10:32, "But call to remembrance the former days, in which, after ye were illuminated, ye endured a great fight of afflictions." The writer of the book of Hebrews is saying, "Remember what you were willing to do to obey God when you were first saved, regardless of what anyone said or did."

What does Jesus tell the church at Sardis to remember? Remember what it was like to have God work in your life. This is so simple, and yet so powerful. Those who have experienced first-hand the power of God in their lives should pass it on to second, third, and fourth generation people. "Let me tell you what God has done for me; here is what I have witnessed." We need to share that. We all have a story.

Revelation 3:3, "Remember therefore how thou hast received and heard, and hold fast, and repent." Think about a dying church. They are not interested in sharing their faith with other people. In fact, if someone new walks through the door, they just stare at them. "Hey Ethel, do you know who that is?" "No Fred, I've never seen them before." I have personally known of people who walked into a church for the first time and not a single person spoke to them, not even the pastor. They are not interested in reaching new people. New people disturb the comfortableness of the funeral parlor they attend every week.

People in a dying church say they believe in a set of Biblical doctrines, but they lack a depth of spiritual understanding. The reason they lack a depth of understanding is because they no longer hunger and thirst after righteousness. Matthew 5:6, "Blessed are they which do hunger and thirst after righteousness: for they shall be filled." In a dying church, people see no need for that. They arrived somewhere around 1993, or 1973, or 2003. Whenever they arrived, they arrived, and they no longer hunger and thirst for God. They believe they have all the spiritual nourishment they will ever need. But in reality, they are dying from spiritual malnutrition.

People in a dying church are very comfortable in their complacency. They are more concerned with their personal comfort than they are with personal conviction and growth. They like a good sermon that really slams everyone else but doesn't upset their applecart. They get all excited when you talk about correcting other people, but they are satisfied with themselves.

What lessons do we learn from Sardis? Be watchful for the return of Jesus Christ, for we know not the day nor the hour when He will return.

~~*Strengthen what you have.*
~~*Remember what God has done in your life.*
~~*Hold fast, don't let go of the truths of God's Word.*
~~*Repent! Repentance is not a one-time experience.*

Revelation 3:4-6; (4) "Thou hast a few names even in Sardis which have not defiled their garments; and they shall walk with Me in white: for they are worthy. (5) He that overcometh, the same shall be clothed in white raiment; and I will not blot out his name out of the book of life, but I will confess his name before My Father, and before His angels. (6) He that hath an ear, let him hear what the Spirit saith unto the churches."

The letter to Sardis is just as much for the church of today as it was to the church of 2,000 years ago. God help us to hear what the Spirit is saying to the church.

Philadelphia

Church number six is Philadelphia, the original city of "brotherly love." Revelation 3:7-13, "(7) And to the angel of the church in Philadelphia write; These things saith He that is holy, He that is true, He that hath the key of David, He that openeth, and no man shutteth; and shutteth, and no man openeth; (8) I know thy works: behold, I have set before thee an open door, and no man can shut it: for thou hast a little strength, and hast kept My Word, and hast not denied My name. (9) Behold, I will make them of the synagogue of satan, which say they are Jews, and are not, but do lie; behold, I will make them to come and worship before thy feet, and to know that I have loved thee. (10) Because thou hast kept the word of My patience, I also will keep thee from the hour of temptation, which shall come upon all the world, to try them that dwell upon the earth. (11) Behold, I come quickly: hold that fast which thou hast, that no man take thy crown. (12) Him that overcometh will I make a pillar in the temple of My God, and he shall go no more out: and I will write upon him the name of My God, and the name of the city of My God, which is new Jerusalem, which cometh down out of heaven from My God: and I will write upon him My new name. (13) He that hath an ear, let him hear what the Spirit saith unto the churches."

Philadelphia was located on a hillside about 30 miles southeast of Sardis. It was founded by Attalus II, the king of Pergamum, around 190 B.C. The town was given the name "Philadelphus," because of the love that Attalus II had for his brother, Eumenes II. The modern name of this town is Allah-shehr, city of God. Philadelphia is the only church out of the seven that doesn't have any words of correction or condemnation spoken against it. Theirs is an uplifting message of hope and encouragement, an appeal to continue what they were already doing.

Revelation 3:7, "And to the angel of the church in Philadelphia write; These things saith He that is holy." Think about some of the Scriptures where we are reminded that God is holy, and how we are called to holiness. Isaiah 43:3, "For I am the Lord thy God, the Holy One of Israel, thy Saviour." Hebrews 12:14, "Follow peace with all men, and holiness, without which no man shall see the Lord." 1 Peter 1:16, "Be ye holy; for I am holy." God is holy, and He requires holiness from us.

Revelation 3:7 goes on to say, "He that hath the key of David, He that openeth, and no man shutteth; and shutteth, and no man openeth." Why is Jesus described as the one who has the key of David? What is the key of David?

Isaiah 22: 15-23, "Thus saith the Lord God of hosts, Go, get thee unto this treasurer, even unto Shebna, which is over the house, and say, (16)

What hast thou here? and whom hast thou here, that thou hast hewed thee out a sepulchre here, as he that heweth him out a sepulchre on high, and that graveth an habitation for himself in a rock? (17) Behold, the Lord will carry thee away with a mighty captivity and will surely cover thee. (18) He will surely violently turn and toss thee like a ball into a large country: there shalt thou die, and there the chariots of thy glory shall be the shame of thy lord's house. (19) And I will drive thee from thy station, and from thy state shall he pull thee down. (20) And it shall come to pass in that day, that I will call my servant Eliakim the son of Hilkiah: (21) And I will clothe him with thy robe, and strengthen him with thy girdle, and I will commit thy government into his hand: and he shall be a father to the inhabitants of Jerusalem, and to the house of Judah. (22) And the key of the house of David will I lay upon his shoulder; so he shall open, and none shall shut; and he shall shut, and none shall open. (23) And I will fasten him as a nail in a sure place; and he shall be for a glorious throne to his father's house."

Isaiah 22:15 tells us about Shebna, a steward who worked for the king. In this position, Shebna determined who had access to the king. It was a position of honor, but in this case, Shebna allowed it to fill him with pride. In verse 16, he builds a kingly tomb, but he builds it for himself. He misuses his authority. Because of his sin, Shebna is replaced by Eliakim who was a godly individual

Eliakim's duties are described in Isaiah 22:21-22, "(21) And I will clothe him with thy robe, and strengthen him with thy girdle, and I will commit thy government into his hand: and he shall be a father to the inhabitants of Jerusalem, and to the house of Judah. (22) And the key of the house of David will I lay upon his shoulder; so he shall open, and none shall shut; and he shall shut, and none shall open."

Keys in ancient times were no different than keys today. They opened doors; they granted access. The steward would be the one who granted access to the king. This key of David is about having the right of entry to the king. Those who served in a position like Eliakim could actually be identified by the clothing they wore. A symbol of a key was embroidered on the shoulder of their garment. When you walked into a room and saw that key, you knew that this was the man who could grant you entrance to the king.

There is another verse of Scripture in Isaiah that you may be more familiar with. Isaiah 9:6-7. "(6) For unto us a Child is born, unto us a Son is given: and the government shall be upon His shoulder: and His name shall be called Wonderful, Counsellor, The mighty God, The everlasting Father, The Prince of Peace. (7) Of the increase of His government and peace there shall be no end, upon the throne of David, and upon his kingdom, to order it, and to establish it with judgment and with justice from henceforth even forever. The zeal of the Lord of hosts will perform this."

Eliakim was a type of Christ in the sense that Jesus is the only one who can grant us access into the kingdom of our God.

Revelation 3:7-8, "(7) And to the angel of the church in Philadelphia write; These things saith He that is holy, He that is true, He that hath the key of David, He that openeth, and no man shutteth; and shutteth, and no man openeth; (8) I know thy works: behold, I have set before thee an open door, and no man can shut it: for thou hast a little strength, and hast kept My Word, and hast not denied My name."

We are looking at two different doors here. The first door is the door of salvation. Jesus is the Holy One of Israel. He is the way, the truth and the life, and no one can have access to the Father except through Him. (John 14:6) Jesus has the keys of David.

But in verse 8, Jesus says that He has set before the church in Philadelphia an open door. What is this open door? Let's look at 2 Corinthians 2:12-13, "(12) Furthermore, when I came to Troas to preach Christ's Gospel, and a door was opened unto me of the Lord, (13) I had no rest in my spirit, because I found not Titus my brother: but taking my leave of them, I went from thence into Macedonia." The

Apostle Paul uses this same idea of an open door to describe something different. As he was on one of his journeys, he says, "a door was opened to me by the Lord." It seems that he was expecting Titus to be in Troas, but he was not, so Paul left for Macedonia. We can read about this Macedonian Call in Acts, chapter 16.

An open door was how Paul expressed the opportunity he had to bring the Gospel to Europe. If we follow that same thought process, Jesus is saying that the church in Philadelphia has an open door to preach the Gospel in their community. And then Jesus adds, "no man can shut it." That is a powerful statement. No man or devil can shut the door that God opens for ministry, whether on a church level or an individual level. Are there any doors that God has ever opened for you?

The common connection between these doors is that they are both opened by Christ, and we must step through them. He opens the door of salvation, and He also opens the door of ministry. But we have a greater involvement in the second door. Jesus is the only one who can bring salvation, but He chooses to use us to spread this "Good News" to the world. It is not because we are so great. If you notice in verse 8, it also says, "you have a little strength." So, it isn't because of our strength.

Two passages of Scripture come to mind. 2 Corinthians 12:9, "And He (Jesus) said unto me, My grace is sufficient for thee: for My strength is made perfect in weakness. Most gladly therefore will I rather glory in my infirmities, that the power of Christ may rest upon me." Paul is describing his lack of strength in the midst of his physical disabilities, but God said to Paul that His grace was sufficient, and that God's strength is made perfect in human weakness. If we think about that in connection to the church in Philadelphia, a little strength would be considered a good characteristic because they evidently realized that they were reliant on the strength of God. There is also the Scripture in Zechariah 4:6, "This is the word of the Lord unto Zerubbabel, saying, Not by might, nor by power, but by My spirit, saith the Lord of hosts." All our help comes from above.

Revelation 3:8 also says, "You have kept My Word." Philadelphia was a church with little strength, but they were keeping the Word. One of the most sobering passages of Scripture in the Bible is found in Matthew 7:21-23, "(21) Not every one that saith unto Me, Lord, Lord, shall enter into the kingdom of heaven; but he that doeth the will of My Father which is in heaven. (22) Many will say to Me in that day, Lord, Lord, have we not prophesied in Thy name? and in Thy name have cast out devils? and in Thy name done many wonderful works? (23) And then will I profess unto them, I never knew you: depart from Me, ye that work iniquity." Those verses should stop us in our tracks and cause us to do some serious soul searching. It is not enough to know God's Word. We have to keep and obey God's Word. It is not enough to know all the right words to say. We must live a holy life. As stated previously, it is possible to be religious but spiritually lost. The church at Philadelphia kept God's Word.

Revelation 3:8 continues, "you have not denied My name." That brings to mind Matthew 10:32-33, "(32) Whosoever therefore shall confess Me before men, him will I confess also before My Father which is in heaven. (33) But whosoever shall deny Me before men, him will I also deny before My Father which is in heaven." We must not be afraid or ashamed to stand up for Jesus. He is the hope of the world, and we must not allow a wicked culture to silence our testimony. James 4:17 says, "Therefore to him that knoweth to do good, and doeth it not, to him it is sin." We must live out our faith.

The church at Philadelphia is doing such a great job that an incredible statement is said about them. Revelation 3:9 says "Behold, I will make them of the synagogue of Satan, which say they are Jews, and are not, but do lie; behold, I will make them to come and worship before thy feet, and to know that I have loved thee." I love this verse. Jesus is saying that the church can live in such a way that unbelievers will have to bow at the feet of the believer. Unbelievers belong to the wrong church. They belong to the synagogue of Satan. The church in

Philadelphia was a powerful church doing a great work in their city.

Revelation 3:10, "Because thou hast kept the word of My patience, I also will keep thee from the hour of temptation, which shall come upon all the world, to try them that dwell upon the earth." Perseverance and endurance are part of being a Christian. What is this hour of temptation that is going to come upon all the world? At first glance, there would seem to be a connection between this verse and verses in Matthew 24:21-22, where we read "(21) For then shall be great tribulation, such as was not since the beginning of the world to this time, no, nor ever shall be. (22) And except those days should be shortened, there should no flesh be saved: but for the elect's sake those days shall be shortened."

How will they be kept from the hour of trial? Does this mean they will not have to experience it at all, or does it mean that they will they be kept through it? Was it describing something that the church in Philadelphia was facing nearly 2,000 years ago, or is it a specific reference to the last days? Either way, Jesus says He will keep us, and that is what we should focus our attention on.

Revelation 3:11, "Behold, I come quickly: hold that fast which thou hast, that no man take thy crown." That word "quickly" can mean something that will happen soon, or it can mean that when it reaches a certain point, there's no stopping it. If those who read this 2,000 years ago thought it meant soon, they were mistaken. They were mistaken just as so many through the years have misunderstood the timetable of the Lord's return. The one thing about which there can be no controversy is this; when His return begins, nothing will stop it.

Jesus tells the church at Philadelphia to "hold fast". They have an open door that no man can shut. They have kept God's Word. They have not denied God's name. And, they have patience. Jesus says, "Hold fast that no one man take your crown." The Greek word that is translated crown here is "stéphanos" which refers to a victor's crown, not "diádēma" which refers to a kingly crown. Jesus says, don't let anything or anyone take that away from you.

In 2 Thessalonians 2:9-10, "(9) Even him, whose coming is after the working of Satan with all power and signs and lying wonders, (10) And with all deceivableness of unrighteousness in them that perish; because they received not the love of the truth, that they might be saved." The Bible tells us that Satan is a thief and a liar. His sole intention is to steal, kill and destroy. As he has done since God created man, Satan sends strong delusions in an effort to cause people to refuse the truth and to reject the love of God. Sadly, we see that all around us today, but it doesn't have to be that way. We can hold fast.

In Revelation 3:12, we see the eternal outcome of holding on to the truths of God. "Him that overcometh will I make a pillar in the temple of My God, and he shall go no more out: and I will write upon him the name of My God, and the name of the city of My God, which is new Jerusalem, which cometh down out of heaven from My God: and I will write upon him My new name."

Jesus speaks of writing three names on those who make it to this New Jerusalem. One is God's Name. Why would you write God's Name on an individual? Well, when someone writes their name on something, it means that it belongs to them? Your Bible probably has your name in it because you want everyone to know it belongs to you. This name signifies we belong to God. He has written His Name on us.

The second name is the name of God's holy city. Philadelphia of old suffered through numerous earthquakes that would often destroy their city. But the New Jerusalem is built by God Himself, and it will never be destroyed. According to this verse, the name of that city is written on us. Why? Because we belong in the New Jerusalem. We have eternal citizenship in the Kingdom and writing the name of God's city on us recognizes that we are no longer a pilgrim and a stranger in a foreign land. We are home.

The third name that's written on the citizens of the New Jerusalem is our new name. We saw this referenced in the letter to the church at Pergamos. It is our new name on a white stone. (Revelation 2:17)

We read in Revelation 3:13, "He that hath an ear, let him hear what the Spirit saith unto the churches." The letter to Philadelphia is an encouraging letter. "Keep it up. Continue to persevere. Continue to grow. Continue to overcome." It is such a powerful, positive message. I think I would like to be counted as a member at Philadelphia, wouldn't you? But, watch out, Laodicea is next...

Laodicea

The final church is located at Laodicea, which is the furthest south of all the churches we have been studying. The church of Laodicea is mentioned five times in the book of Colossians with Colossians 4:16 telling us that Paul had written a letter to them, just as he did to Colossae. "And when this epistle is read among you, cause that it be read also in the church of the Laodiceans; and that ye likewise read the epistle from Laodicea." Colossians 1:1-7, would seem to indicate that Epaphras founded the church at Colossae which was about ten miles from Laodicea. That being the case, it is at least conceivable that he would also be responsible for planting the church at Laodicea although there is no historical evidence to support that. The pastor of Laodicea is thought to have been Archippus, whom Paul warned to be diligent in fulfilling his ministry. Colossians 4:17, "And say to Archippus, take heed to the ministry which thou hast received in the Lord, that thou fulfil it."

Revelation 3:14-22, "(14) And unto the angel of the church of the Laodiceans write; These things saith the Amen, the faithful and true witness, the beginning of the creation of God; (15) I know thy works, that thou art neither cold nor hot: I would thou wert cold or hot. (16) So then because thou art lukewarm, and neither cold nor hot, I will spue thee out of My mouth. (17) Because thou sayest, I am rich, and increased with goods, and have need of nothing; and knowest not that thou art wretched, and miserable, and poor, and blind, and naked: (18) I counsel thee to buy of Me gold tried in the fire, that thou mayest be rich; and white raiment, that thou mayest be clothed, and that the shame of thy nakedness doth not appear; and anoint thine eyes with eyesalve, that thou mayest see. (19) As many as I love, I rebuke and chasten: be zealous therefore, and repent. (20) Behold, I stand at the door, and knock: if any man hear My voice, and open the door, I will come in to him, and will sup with him, and he with Me. (21) To him that overcometh will I grant to sit with Me in my throne, even as I also overcame, and am set down with My Father in His throne. (22) He that hath an ear, let him hear what the Spirit saith unto the churches."

Let's look at Laodicea from the historical context of the churches in Asia Minor. These seven churches were probably started as a result of the time that the Apostle Paul spent in Ephesus which is recorded in the book of Acts. There were almost certainly many other churches in this area, but these are the seven that were singled out in the book of Revelation. Laodicea was about 45 miles southeast of the city of Philadelphia and about 100 miles east of Ephesus. The city was rebuilt by Antiochus II and named for his wife, Laodice, around 260 B.C. It was a center for trade and commerce. There were large amounts of gold stored there. Laodicea was famous for its high-quality black wool. This, plus other business ventures, made it one of the wealthiest cities in the Roman Empire. Nothing remains today except ruins. It is known today as Eski-hissar, or "old castle."

The book of Revelation was written during the reign of the Roman emperor Domitian. Numerous writers who lived during that time have documented how Domitian declared himself to be "Lord and God." This insulted Christians, Jews and the Roman Senate alike. Domitian persecuted those who would not participate in worshipping him. Although the Jews were exempt from the requirements of emperor worship, Christians were not. Thus, the Christians at Laodicea were affected by Domitian's decrees. Their response to this persecution, which also involved their ability to buy and sell, is what caused Jesus to respond to this church with such condemnation.

The culture of 2,000 years ago placed great difficulties upon the Christians. Those who refused to worship the image of the emperor were killed. The pressure upon wealthy Christians to maintain their wealth was intense. Since a great deal of Laodicea's wealth depended upon trade, the Christian merchants were in a predicament. Would they cooperate and maintain their trade associations, or would they renounce Domitian and reaffirm their faith in Christ? Many of the Laodicean Christians compromised their faith to such an extent that Jesus said in verse 16, "I will vomit you out of my mouth." As we have seen, other churches responded differently. The Christians at Smyrna maintained their faith in the midst of extreme difficulty by refusing to participate in emperor worship even though this meant affliction and poverty for them. (Revelation 2:9)

If you own a business, you have to provide a good product, serve your customer, take care of them, develop a relationship of trust, and do those things consistently in order to prosper. That's the nature of business. Sometimes you are faced with the temptation to follow some questionable business practices that are commonplace in the world. You are pressured to overlook certain things that you perhaps might not ordinarily approve of in order to maintain the business. In some cases, the unethical practices move into the illegal. Laodicea became everything to everyone. It was neither hot nor cold, but it prospered. They thought the end justified the means. We have seen this over and over throughout history, and it certainly has come to the forefront in recent years where our current culture is trying to force everyone to fit into the liberal mindset of what is socially and politically correct by worldly standards. Many of us grew up during a time when the standards of society so closely resembled the standards of our faith that there was no conflict between the two. Those days are gone, and the pressures on business owners today is to conform. What does Jesus tell the church of Laodicea to do? He says, "Repent!"

How much of this has seeped into our lives so that we can more easily fit in with the world of the 21st century? Laodicea existed at the height of the Roman Empire, and these cities had to accommodate themselves to Rome and the order it brought. The people in Laodicea were surrounded by pagan cultures, and it was a very hard world in which to live. We're beginning to see some of that in our day as our American culture is rapidly changing.

A major earthquake struck this area in 17 A.D. and destroyed most of Laodicea. At that time, the entire region was a part of the Roman Empire, but Laodicea did not need any FEMA (government disaster) aid. They had enough money so they rebuilt on their own, which again gets to the point that Jesus makes when He says, "You're rich and increased in goods, and have need of nothing." They had enough money that they didn't need government assistance to rebuild their city after a devastating earthquake. That is quite a statement of their financial independence.

Historically, there were no interesting features about the city. Remember Pergamos, they had a huge mountain on which the city was built. Ephesus was a great harbor city like Smyrna. Laodicea did have a famous school of medicine. You may remember that I mentioned a man named Galen in our study on the church at Pergamos. He was one of the foremost doctors of the ancient world and is sometimes referred to as the father of medical science. He writes about a "Phrygian Powder" for which the medical school of Laodicea seems to have been famous. This ointment, or salve, was known for its healing abilities for eye defects, which is again why Jesus says, "I encourage you to buy some eye salve to remove your blindness". Of course, Jesus was speaking spiritually and not physically, but they would have understood this reference because of the Phrygian Powder that was associated with Laodicea.

The Romans engineered aqueducts wherever they went. Almost unbelievably, there are some aqueducts which were built over 2,000 years ago that continue to transport water today, especially in Italy. In the case of Laodicea, there was an aqueduct that brought water into the city from the cool springs near Colossae and also from the hot springs near Hierapolis. By the time the water got to Laodicea from either location, it was lukewarm.

A little-known fact about the Laodicean church is that its "lukewarm" title would not be its final legacy. The church at Laodicea survived Domitian's reign. The city became what is known as a "Bishopric" or the place of a Christian Bishop. A Christian Council was held there in the fourth century. Archaeologists have discovered about 20 ancient Christian chapels and churches at this site. The largest church at Laodicea, called the Church of Laodicea, took up an entire city block and dates to the beginning of the fourth century.

In verse 17, we are given some insight as to how the church at Laodicea saw itself. "Thou sayest, I am rich, and increased with goods, and have need of nothing." How did Jesus respond to that? "(17) you don't even know that you are wretched, and miserable, and poor, and blind, and naked: (18) I counsel thee to buy of Me gold tried in the fire, that thou mayest be rich; and white raiment, that thou mayest be clothed, and that the shame of thy nakedness do not appear; and anoint thine eyes with eyesalve, that thou mayest see. (19) As many as I love, I rebuke and chasten: be zealous therefore, and repent. (20) Behold, I stand at the door, and knock: if any man hear My voice, and open the door, I will come in to him, and will sup with him, and he with Me."

The harshest criticism given to any church is given to Laodicea, but a great truth that is often overlooked is found in verse 19. Jesus said He is speaking to them this way because He loves them. That gets lost in much of the modern church. This truth is also stated in Hebrews 12:6, "For whom the Lord loveth he chasteneth." When preachers today preach what is deemed a strong message, they are accused of not loving people. And I will admit that some of them probably don't. But the meanest thing we can ever do as a minister of the Gospel, or as a Christian for that matter, is to fail to sound the alarm when we see impending destruction coming. Ezekiel chapter 33:6 says, "But if the watchman see the sword come, and blow not the trumpet, and the people be not warned; if the sword come, and take any person from among them, he is taken away in his iniquity; but his blood will I require at the watchman's hand." We are watchmen on a wall. We bear a great responsibility.

The cultural impact on Laodicea seems to have lulled the Laodicean congregation into self-deception, and that is what Christ is pointing out as being very dangerous. They didn't know they were naked before God. They were members of the church. They had a place to fellowship each week, very likely in a member's home based on what Paul said in Colossians chapter 4. Whatever the church was doing in Laodicea, they were a part of it. But Jesus saw something they didn't see. He saw through their bank accounts, their clothing, their chrome-plated chariots parked outside the home where they met. He saw through the lifestyle they were living for what it truly was, and He saw what it was doing to them.

These people attended all the functions of the church. They went to all the special activities. They went to the men's and women's retreats. And yet, Jesus says that they were miserable, poor, blind, and naked. This lukewarm state is nauseating to God. Jesus didn't want them to fall away, but He did want them to be authentic. Jesus wanted them to be useful. He wanted to do His work in them just as He does with us today. This is the whole point of Jesus telling them that He is standing at the door. "I'm standing at the door knocking. Let Me come in and fellowship with you."

The Laodiceans were blind to their condition, and as a result they said, "we are rich and increased with goods, and have need of nothing." That is a disturbingly accurate description of our world today. At the most affluent period of human history, we live in a world where people do not need God. They literally do not need Him. They do not need the message of the Kingdom of God because they have their own "kingdoms." They do not need the healing power of God because they have good insurance. They have enough money. They can do whatever they want. They can buy whatever they want. They can build whatever they want. They can go wherever they want. And for many, all of that cost is just pocket change.

The message to Laodicea is showing us that the spirit of the surrounding culture can creep into the congregation, and it can paralyze our spiritual life. That is something we all should think about and consider as we look at this message. How much of today's culture has crept into us, into the church? And how much does it cause us to be blind, miserable, poor, and naked before God? That is the question we should talk about.

Jesus say in verse 18, "(18) I counsel thee to buy of Me gold tried in the fire, that thou mayest be rich; and white raiment, that thou mayest be clothed, and that the shame of thy nakedness do not appear; and anoint thine eyes with eyesalve, that thou mayest see." There are three things here that Jesus encourages them to buy. The first is gold that has been tried in the fire. As a wealthy city, Laodicea had large deposits of gold. But Jesus was talking about spiritual gold; a life of character, a life of change, a life of overcoming whatever the world throws at us. Even when we suffer, even when we have to bind up our wounds, we will not deny God. We will not reject the faith. We will be faithful. And the end result is that our character and our quality can be finer than the finest gold. This is what Jesus says to buy.

Secondly, we are to "Buy some white garments that you may be clothed, so that the shame of your nakedness may not be revealed." The book of Revelation shows us that white garments are symbols of righteousness. It's turning the other cheek when it goes against your grain. It's keeping your tongue when you want to go marching in and tell somebody off. It is the putting on of a garment of trust, of faith and of patience. These are the things we have to buy through hard earned, hard fought effort. These things are bought by living a righteous life in the world today. He's telling us to put that on.

The third thing is to anoint your eyes so you can see. Buy a salve that really works, not this Phrygian Powder stuff. Open your eyes so you can see the things that have caused your deception. He wanted them to see the gold, the clothing and wool that was a part of their trade culture, and the Phrygian Powder. Jesus uses these three things to point out the need for the Laodiceans to live an authentic life without blinders. See the rich possibilities of a living completely surrendered to God. This is what He is telling them to buy.

We can look to false hopes. We can look to false heroes to gain our identity, to gain our sense of worth and fulfillment. But ultimately, we have to get to the point where we look to Christ for that. This is what Jesus is wanting those who are caught up in this Laodicean spirit to do. Look to Him and not to the fabricated idols of a society. What should we do if we find ourselves in such a situation as the Laodiceans? Jesus says in verse 19, "As many as I love, I rebuke and chasten. Therefore, be zealous and repent." The only way out of the spirit of Laodicea is repentance. What is your tolerance level for the popular culture and its subsequent impact? Make no mistake, it does impact us, and we are the only ones who can answer that question of what we should do.

We have reached a point in the 21st century where this profane spirit has crept in to the church, and we should acknowledge that. It has crept into our nation at the highest level. America is moving headlong toward its Roman roots. The morality of our current world is a society that has rejected God and does not want to keep God in its knowledge. It's in the headlines every day. In Romans chapter 1, Paul says that it is possible to reject God to such an extent that people no longer want to retain God in their knowledge, and as a result, God gives them over to a reprobate mind. He was not only describing the world of the 1st century, He was describing the world of our day. We have experienced a removal of God from our public forum. When I was a young man, the Supreme Court ruled that abortion was legal, and since then over 60 million abortions have been performed. The latest intrusion with the same sex ruling is just one more example of a culture at its highest level that does not want to retain God and His knowledge as the foundation of our laws. The trans-gender and multi-gender issues which are surfacing now are quite frankly impossible to understand to reasonable thinking people, but many who have had their conscience seared see nothing wrong with it. Reprobate minds!

You can quote any news agency that makes you feel good, but the root of the problem is that our leaders in America are spiritually drunk. The Prophet Hosea describes the nation of Judah as reaching this condition because of idolatry." Hosea 4:1-2 says "(1) there is no truth, nor mercy, nor knowledge of God in the land. (2) By swearing, and lying, and killing, and stealing, and committing adultery, they break out, and blood toucheth blood." A rejection of God had caused them to remove the landmarks that show people what the standards were and how to walk in them. Those landmarks have been removed in our beloved nation as well. America is walking blindly along the road indulging in a sinful culture because leadership has removed the landmarks. We don't need to quote anyone other than the prophets like Hosea and Isaiah to get to the real reason we are witnessing the things that are happening in our nation today.

Whatever your political stance may be, the news media today is totally out of control. Our culture and our society are drunk spiritually because of idolatry and the breaking of God's commandments and God's law. The Scriptures clearly show that this creates a blindness and an inability to truly lead and to stand for righteousness. It gets to the point where good is called evil, and evil is called good. This is where we are today. Many religious leaders don't even know how to look at some issues because they have surrendered to political correctness. They have sold their soul for fame, riches and popularity. They have a corrupt theology because of a refusal to accept what the Scriptures say.

Jesus is saying to His Church, "don't be blind and naked and poor and miserable. Repent." The message to Laodicea is a clarion call to all of us to look and examine ourselves. Jesus is pointing the finger at us. And if need be, we have the opportunity to repent and open the door so that Jesus can come in and dine with us. If we don't do that, then we are just like the church at Laodicea. Jesus is standing at the door. He is looking, and He is knocking. The question is, "Will we open the door and let Him come in?" One day, Jesus is coming back for His church, a church without spot or blemish. I want to be a part of that church. How about you?

Revelation 3:20 is one of the saddest verses in the Bible. This church that thinks they have everything has locked Jesus out of His own church. Their attitude seems to have been, "we have everything we need, so we don't need Jesus."

The message to the church at Laodicea was direct and unyielding. As Jesus dealt with various issues in these churches, we see that five of the previous churches had some good and some bad. Philadelphia had only good, but Laodicea had only bad. Jesus could say these things to them because He knows the heart. When you hear the word "Laodicea" today, it is seldom followed with anything good being said about it. To a certain extent, you can understand that. But, may I remind you that Laodicea probably started out as a good church. This letter is a warning to what can happen to any church that basically locks Jesus out.

If there is one positive note that you can squeeze out of this letter to Laodicea, it is found in verse 21-22, "(21) To him that overcometh will I grant to sit with Me in my throne. (22) He that hath an ear, let him hear what the Spirit saith unto the churches." That's a pretty close relationship that Jesus is offering them. He is saying that even in Laodicea there is a possibility to overcome. There is a possibility to sit down in the Kingdom with Jesus if they will only hear what the Spirit is saying.

These seven churches of Revelation that John could send letters to literally existed 2,000 years ago. They area where they were located is modern day Turkey which today is 99.8% Muslim. This tells me that, over a period of time, they failed to pass along their faith to the next generation. These messages to the seven churches in Revelation have always applied to all churches, no matter when or where they existed. To assign them to a certain time frame or dispensation is Biblically wrong. Every one of these churches offers a lesson for us to apply to our lives today. In every church, there can be passionate people for Christ sitting next to people who have grown lukewarm. There can be people holding onto doctrinal truths exactly as the Scripture teaches sitting alongside some who may refuse to accept the truth. As Jesus has shown us in the letters to these churches, you can have the name of being a Christian but not be right with God. The question we need to ask ourselves is this, "Which church am I a member of?"

IV
The Great and Terrible Day of the Lord

Rapture, no rapture, Pre-trib, Mid-trib, Post-trib, Second Coming. I have listened to people argue this all my life. I wonder if God ever looks down at us and just shakes His head. We major on the minors and have so confused the most elementary truths that unbelievers are left totally befuddled, and oftentimes even those who go to church are confused. While I'm sure that these discussions will continue until the Lord comes back, may I suggest to you that there is something far more important that we should concern ourselves with. It is the most basic issue of life; am I ready to die right now? Millions have died thinking they would see the return of the Lord, but they died, and Jesus still has not returned. Each of us is just one heartbeat away from death. What then? Where will we spend eternity? I enjoy discussing the timing of the Lord's return as much as anyone, but it is more critically important that I am ready to meet the Lord at any given moment. Are you ready to die?

Over the past few years, we have heard so much about these blood moons. Every time we have one, it is used as an indicator of the last days, and modern-day Balaams use fear to manipulate people. Perhaps the greatest argument for the rapture is found in the gap between the end of chapter 3 and the opening verse of chapter 4 in the book of Revelation. The first three chapters are devoted to the church on earth, but when you enter chapter 4, the church is not mentioned as being on earth again. Some say this is proof that we will not have to suffer through the tribulation. If the only reason you believe in the pre-trib rapture of the church is so you will escape tribulation, that is a slap in the face to the millions of Christians who have suffered and who have been put to death for the past two thousand years, and to those who are still being persecuted and slaughtered around the world today.

While I have my own thoughts as to how the end days could possibly play out, I can't begin to stress what I've already mentioned a couple of times in this study. Millions have died who expected the Lord to return in their lifetime, but He didn't. What we can count on is this, Hebrews 9:27, "It is appointed unto man once to die, but after this the judgment." The most important thing is to be ready to meet the Lord, whenever and however the last days unfold.

As was mentioned at the beginning of our study of the book of Revelation, this book is a little easier to understand if we break it down into three basic sections; that which was, that which is; that which is to come. It is clearly spelled out in Revelation 1:19, "Write the things which thou hast seen, and the things which are, and the things which shall be hereafter." "What was" is found in chapter 1, "what is" is found in chapters 2 and 3, and "what will be" is found from chapter 4 through chapter 22. Join with me now as we begin to look at "what is yet to be".

V
Chapters 4-22

Revelation: Chapter 4

Revelation 4:1-4, "(1) After this I looked, and, behold, a door was opened in heaven: and the first voice which I heard was as it were of a trumpet talking with me; which said, Come up hither, and I will shew thee things which must be hereafter. (2) And immediately I was in the spirit: and, behold, a throne was set in heaven, and One sat on the throne. (3) And He that sat was to look upon like a jasper and a sardine stone: and there was a rainbow round about the throne, in sight like unto an emerald. (4) And round about the throne were four and twenty seats: and upon the seats I saw four and twenty elders sitting, clothed in white raiment; and they had on their heads crowns of gold."

Who are these twenty-four elders? In one of my sermons, I have speculated on these twenty-four elders and who they might be. Let me remind you of my definition of "speculation". Simply stated, it means "I can't prove what I'm about to say is true, but you can't prove that it's not." I think that would clear up a lot of misunderstanding on many Scriptures if we could just accept 1 Corinthians 13:12, "For now we see through a glass, darkly; but then face to face: now I know in part; but then shall I know even as also I am known."

In my research. I came across several differing opinions as to who the twenty-four elders could be so I'm adding my thoughts to what many others have said. I would suggest that twelve of the twenty-four represent the Old Covenant. You could say the twelve tribes of Israel, but I prefer the broader expanse of the entire Old Covenant that is the foundation for the entire Old Testament. It was God's revealed plan that was first spoken in Genesis chapter 3 and then set forth under the Law. The twelve tribes may represent that. If so, I suppose we should go back to the original twelve sons of Jacob instead of the redefined twelve tribes when Levi was eliminated from possessing any land once they entered the Promised Land, and when Joseph was removed, and his two sons took his place. In other words, remove Levi and Joseph from the original twelve sons of Jacob and add Manasseh and Ephraim. If twelve of these elders are the twelve tribes of Israel, then you have to clarify which twelve.

If twelve of these elders in chapter 4 do, in fact. represent the Old Covenant, then it is only logical that the other twelve represent the New Covenant. Here again, some have said the twelve Apostles. If that is true, we know it can't be the original twelve because Judas was in the original set, so it would be the revised twelve that had Matthias being chosen as the one to replace Judas in Acts chapter 1. Some would remove Matthias from the list and add Paul. I read where one scholar tried to justify the premise that I just set forth by referencing the Scripture in Revelation 21:12-14, "(12) And had a wall great and high, and had twelve gates, and at the gates twelve angels, and names written thereon, which are the names of the twelve tribes of the children of Israel: (13) On the east three gates; on the north three gates; on the south three gates; and on the west three gates. (14) And the wall of the city had twelve foundations, and in them the names of the twelve apostles of the Lamb." To use those verses to prove who the twenty-four elders are seems a bit of a stretch. There's no denying that the names of the twelve tribes are written of the gates, and the names of the twelve Apostles are written on the foundation, but what does that have to do with the twenty-four elders? Again, I prefer the broader expanse of saying that these twelve represent the entire New Covenant which represents the New Testament Church.

Some people try to make the book of Revelation so confusing that no one can understand it. God is not trying to hide what is truly important to us. He's showing us what we need to know. We tend to waste too much time on all the non-essentials when the most important is standing right in front of us. The bottom line is this; all our speculation is just that, "speculation". I can cite numerous well-known and trusted Bible scholars who all have different opinions on this subject. Several years ago, I heard a well-known evangelist say that he just might be one of these elders. We will find out who these twenty-four elders are when we all get to heaven.

Revelation 4:5-8, "(5) And out of the throne proceeded lightnings and thunderings and voices: and there were seven lamps of fire burning before the throne, which are the seven Spirits of God. (6) And before the throne there was a sea of glass like unto crystal: and in the midst of the throne, and round about the throne, were four beasts full of eyes before and behind. (7) And the first beast was like a lion, and the second beast like a calf, and the third beast had a face as a man, and the fourth beast was like a flying eagle. (8) And the four beasts had each of them six wings about him; and they were full of eyes within: and they rest not day and night, saying, Holy, holy, holy, Lord God Almighty, which was, and is, and is to come."

Ezekiel saw these four creatures in chapter 1 of his writings, and Daniel saw them in chapter 7 of his writings. I have also speculated about who these four beasts are. Although I'm not quite so confident with my assumption of them, I do believe there is some validity to it. I have said that these four beasts represent the four-fold ministry of Christ. The lion, the ox, the man and the eagle. Many times, in the Bible. the lion is used to represent kingship, the ox is used to represent servanthood, the face of a man would obviously represent humanity and the eagle represents deity. In Matthew, we see Jesus as a King. In Mark, we see Jesus as a servant. In Luke, we see Jesus as the Son of man. And in John, we see Jesus as the Son of God. One thing is certain. These four beasts cannot be Christ Himself, so at best they would have to be a representative of the fullness of His ministry.

If there is any validity to my speculating, then what we see is the entire plan of salvation standing around the throne. What began with the Old Covenant and was fulfilled with the New Covenant because of the ministry of Jesus, are all standing around the throne. If it is possible to break the complexity of the Scriptures down to one statement, it would be this; "The theme of the Bible is redemption and what God has done to save fallen man." The Old Testament looked for it, and the New Testament saw the reality of it, all because of the finished work of Christ. The Bible is the story of salvation. Sin is the conflict. Redemption is the theme.

Revelation 4:9-11, "(9) And when those beasts give glory and honour and thanks to Him that sat on the throne, who liveth for ever and ever, (10) The four and twenty elders fall down before Him that sat on the throne, and worship Him that liveth for ever and ever, and cast their crowns before the throne, saying, (11) Thou art worthy, O Lord, to receive glory and honour and power: for Thou hast created all things, and for Thy pleasure they are and were created."

Herein lies the danger of all our debating and trying to figure out who these elders and beasts are. It takes away from the most important element of this scene which is not about the elders nor about the beasts. It is all about the One who sits on the throne. We are given a glimpse of God, and what do we do? We spend all our time trying to figure who these entities are around the throne. The very thing that I just did in this writing. I purposely did this to illustrate what often happens. This is a perfect example of our majoring on the minors and missing the most important. For that reason, my speculating will be greatly diminished from this point forward. We will focus most of our attention on the greater truth contained in the Scriptures, and we will speak less of those things we may never understand.

Verses 9 through 11 present us with an incredible image. The Throne of God in heaven, and from that throne and around that throne are flashes of lightning, rolls of thunder, and the four beasts who never cease to say, "Holy, holy, holy, Lord God Almighty, which was, and is, and is to come." The twenty-four elders join in saying, "Thou art worthy, O Lord, to receive glory and honour and power: for Thou hast created all things, and for Thy pleasure they are and were created." Whoever these elders are and whatever they represent is put into perspective when they take their crowns and cast them at the feet of God. It is a vivid reminder that it is not about us. It is all about God. Makes you want to shout, doesn't it? And this is just the introduction to what is yet to be.

Revelation: Chapter 5

In chapter 5:1-14, the preview of what is going to happen some day continues. "(1) And I saw in the right hand of Him that sat on the throne a book written within and on the backside, sealed with seven seals. (2) And I saw a strong angel proclaiming with a loud voice, Who is worthy to open the book, and to loose the seals thereof? (3) And no man in heaven, nor in earth, neither under the earth, was able to open the book, neither to look thereon. (4) And I wept much, because no man was found worthy to open and to read the book, neither to look thereon. (5) And one of the elders saith unto me, Weep not: behold, the Lion of the tribe of Judah, the Root of David, hath prevailed to open the book, and to loose the seven seals thereof. (6) And I beheld, and, lo, in the midst of the throne and of the four beasts, and in the midst of the elders, stood a Lamb as it had been slain, having seven horns and seven eyes, which are the seven Spirits of God sent forth into all the earth. (7) And he came and took the book out of the right hand of Him that sat upon the throne. (8) And when he had taken the book, the four beasts and four and twenty elders fell down before the Lamb, having every one of them harps, and golden vials full of odours, which are the prayers of saints. (9) And they sung a new song, saying, Thou art worthy to take the book, and to open the seals thereof: for Thou wast slain, and hast redeemed us to God by Thy blood out of every kindred, and tongue, and people, and nation; (10) And hast made us unto our God kings and priests: and we shall reign on the earth. (11) And I beheld, and I heard the voice of many angels round about the throne and the beasts and the elders: and the number of them was ten thousand times ten thousand, and thousands of thousands; (12) Saying with a loud voice, Worthy is the Lamb that was slain to receive power, and riches, and wisdom, and strength, and honour, and glory, and blessing. (13) And every creature which is in heaven, and on the earth, and under the earth, and such as are in the sea, and all that are in them, heard I saying, Blessing, and honour, and glory, and power, be unto Him that sitteth upon the throne, and unto the Lamb for ever and ever. (14) And the four beasts said, Amen. And the four and twenty elders fell down and worshipped Him that liveth for ever and ever."

As John is gazing through heaven's open door, he sees a book that needs to be opened. But there is no one who can open it. There is no one in heaven, no one on earth, and no one under the earth who is worthy to open the book. When John sees this, it causes him to weep. But then, one of the elders speaks to John and urges him to take a second look. When he looks a second time, John sees that the Lion of the tribe of Judah has prevailed and is able to open the book. With seamless transition, the Lion of the tribe of Judah becomes the Lamb who was slain, and all of heaven begins to rejoice. You see, heaven understands that it's all about the Lamb.

"(12) Worthy is the Lamb that was slain to receive power, and riches, and wisdom, and strength, and honour, and glory, and blessing. (13) And every creature which is in heaven, and on the earth, and under the earth, and such as are in the sea, and all that are in them, heard I saying, Blessing, and honour, and glory, and power, be unto Him that sitteth upon the throne, and unto the Lamb for ever and ever. (14) And the four beasts said, Amen. And the four and twenty elders fell down and worshipped Him that liveth for ever and ever."

Many people read verse 11 and interpret it to be saying that the number mentioned here is those who are saved, the redeemed. But read verse 11 again. "And I beheld, and I heard the voice of many angels round about the throne and the beasts and the elders: and the number of them was ten thousand times ten thousand, and thousands of thousands." Now granted, if these elders do indeed represent the redeemed of all ages, then this number which cannot be calculated does include those who accepted the sacrifice of the Lamb and are enjoying the reward of the faithful. Whoever these are who comprise this multitude, they are praising and worshipping the Lamb. That is what we must not overlook. They are worshipping the One who made salvation possible. Revelation chapters 4 and 5 are shouting ground. Imagine what a grand and glorious day that will be.

Revelation: Chapter 6

The book of Revelation and the book of Daniel almost have to be read and studied at the same time because they are dealing with the same events. Daniel 10:1-2, "(1) In the third year of Cyrus king of Persia a thing was revealed unto Daniel, whose name was called Belteshazzar; and the thing was true, but the time appointed was long: and he understood the thing and had understanding of the vision. (2) In those days I Daniel was mourning three full weeks."

Daniel saw what John saw. It was so horrific that Daniel mourned for three weeks, and he didn't eat anything. Daniel 12:9 says, "Go thy way, Daniel: for the words are closed up and sealed till the time of the end."

What was it that Daniel and John saw? Joel 2:31 says, "The sun shall be turned into darkness, and the moon into blood, before the great and terrible day of the Lord come." In Acts 2:20, the Apostle Peter quoted those exact words from the prophet Joel. Malachi 4:5 uses the expression, "the great and terrible day of the Lord."

So, what is the "Great and Terrible Day of the Lord"? We can now see what Daniel and John saw. Revelation 6:1-8, "(1) And I saw when the Lamb opened one of the seals, and I heard, as it were the noise of thunder, one of the four beasts saying, Come and see. (2) And I saw and behold a white horse: and he that sat on him had a bow; and a crown was given unto him: and he went forth conquering, and to conquer. (3) And when He had opened the second seal, I heard the second beast say, Come and see. (4) And there went out another horse that was red: and power was given to him that sat thereon to take peace from the earth, and that they should kill one another: and there was given unto him a great sword. (5) And when He had opened the third seal, I heard the third beast say, Come and see. And I beheld, and lo a black horse; and he that sat on him had a pair of balances in his hand. (6) And I heard a voice in the midst of the four beasts say, A measure of wheat for a penny, and three measures of barley for a penny; and see thou hurt not the oil and the wine. (7) And when He had opened the fourth seal, I heard the voice of the fourth beast say, Come and see. (8) And I looked and behold a pale horse: and his name that sat on him was Death, and Hell followed with him. And power was given unto them over the fourth part of the earth, to kill with sword, and with hunger, and with death, and with the beasts of the earth."

The Four Horsemen of the Apocalypse are unleashed upon the world. The first horse, the white horse, brings a forced peace. In the book of Daniel, a timetable of events is established which Daniel refers to as a period of seventy weeks of seven. That is a total of four hundred and ninety years. Of those seventy weeks, sixty-nine have already been fulfilled. Let's look at that. Daniel 9:24-27, "(24) Seventy weeks are determined upon thy people and upon thy holy city, to finish the transgression, and to make an end of sins, and to make reconciliation for iniquity, and to bring in everlasting righteousness, and to seal up the vision and prophecy, and to anoint the most Holy. (25) Know therefore and understand, that from the going forth of the commandment to restore and to build Jerusalem unto the Messiah the Prince shall be seven weeks, and threescore and two weeks: the street shall be built again, and the wall, even in troublous times. (26) And after threescore and two weeks shall Messiah be cut off, but not for Himself: and the people of the prince that shall come shall destroy the city and the sanctuary; and the end thereof shall be with a flood, and unto the end of the war desolations are determined. (27) And he shall confirm the covenant with many for one week: and in the midst of the week he shall cause the sacrifice and the oblation to cease, and for the overspreading of abominations he shall make it desolate, even until the consummation, and that determined shall be poured upon the desolate."

This vision is actually broken into three time periods. The first week of seven equals forty-nine years. From the time that Daniel was given this vision, it was forty-nine years later when Artaxerxes, King of Persia, issued his decree for the rebuilding of the walls of Jerusalem and the rebuilding of the Temple. We read that in Nehemiah 2:7-9, "(7) Moreover I said unto the king, If it please the king, let letters be given me to the governors beyond the river, that they may convey me over till I come into Judah; (8) And a letter unto Asaph the keeper of the king's forest, that he may give me timber to make beams for the gates of the palace which appertained to the house, and for the wall of the city, and for the house that I shall enter into. And the king granted me, according to the good hand of my God upon me. (9) Then I came to the governors beyond the river and gave them the king's letters. Now the king had sent captains of the army and horsemen with me."

The second time period is sixty-two weeks of seven, for a total of four hundred and thirty-four years. From the time of the rebuilding of the Temple until the death of the Messiah was four hundred and thirty-four years. Of the four hundred and ninety years of Daniel's vision, four hundred and eighty-three have been fulfilled.

At this point, there is a pause in the time frame. It is that pause or the unknown period of time between the crucifixion, resurrection and ascension of Jesus, that everyone tries to figure out. When will Jesus return? The early church thought He would surely come in their lifetime. So much so that the Apostle Peter dealt with that in 2 Peter chapter 3, and the Apostle Paul dealt with it in 2 Timothy. When will the last week of seven occur? It is that last seven years that we are considering in this study which, even for us, is still somewhere in the future. It is part of the vision that Jesus told John in chapter 1 that is yet to be. One thing of which there can be no doubt is that when this day comes, whenever that day may be, it will come quickly, like a flood.

We know there will be wars and rumors of wars. From the time of Christ until today, this world has been in continual war. Having said that, it is in Daniel 9:27 where a covenant is mentioned, a time of peace. You thought I had forgotten about that first horseman, didn't you? This peace will achieve what heretofore has been impossible. There will be peace with Israel and with her enemies. It will last for three and a half years. At the end of the three and a half years, the person who achieved the peace will be the same one who is responsible for breaking the peace.

The second horse of the Apocalypse, the red horse, begins when the Antichrist sets up an image of himself in the Temple and proclaims himself to be God. It is the beginning of an all-out world war. It is the abomination of desolation that Daniel spoke about in chapter 9 and that Jesus spoke about in Matthew chapter 24. There are some who think this has already been fulfilled. In 167 B.C. a Greek ruler by the name of Antiochus Epiphanies erected an altar to Zeus over the altar of burnt offerings in the Temple in Jerusalem, and he also sacrificed a pig on the altar in the Temple. This is clearly not what Daniel and John saw, but it was a terrible time for the Jewish people.

The third horse of the Apocalypse, the black horse, brings famine. This famine is a result of the massive war that is being fought.

The fourth horse of the Apocalypse, the pale horse, brings death. The consequences of the fourth horse are the inevitable results of the war that began with the second horse. Death, whether by sword, or by famine, or by pestilence or by wild beasts, always follows war and famine. The results are disastrous. Twenty-five percent of the world's population will die.

Revelation 6:9-11, "(9) And when He had opened the fifth seal, I saw under the altar the souls of them that were slain for the word of God, and for the testimony which they held: (10) And they cried with a loud voice, saying, How long, O Lord, holy and true, dost thou not judge and avenge our blood on them that dwell on the earth? (11) And white robes were given unto every one of them; and it was said unto them, that they should rest yet for a little season, until their fellow servants also and their brethren, that should be killed as they were, should be fulfilled."

As a minister, I have heard this cry from many people, and, quite frankly, there have been a few times when I cried out myself. "How long, O Lord?" When it looks like everything that could go wrong has gone wrong, when you find yourself falsely accused, when you find your body racked with pain and disease, and the list goes on. There are times when the deep part of us cries out for peace, for relief. "How long, O Lord?"

Revelation 6:12-17, "(12) And I beheld when He had opened the sixth seal, and, lo, there was a great earthquake; and the sun became black as sackcloth of hair, and the moon became as blood; (13) And the stars of heaven fell unto the earth, even as a fig tree casteth her untimely figs, when she is shaken of a mighty wind. (14) And the heaven departed as a scroll when it is rolled together; and every mountain and island were moved out of their places. (15) And the kings of the earth, and the great men, and the rich men, and the chief captains, and the mighty men, and every bondman, and every free man, hid themselves in the dens and in the rocks of the mountains; (16) And said to the mountains and rocks, Fall on us, and hide us from the face of him that sitteth on the throne, and from the wrath of the Lamb: (17) For the great day of his wrath is come; and who shall be able to stand?"

These verses are talking about a time of massive destruction. A few years ago, a book entitled, "The Four Blood Moons," was published. I must confess I was torn between amazement and amusement during that time. Most Christians who believe in the pre-tribulation rapture all agree that it has to take place at the end of Revelation chapter 3 and the beginning of chapter 4, because the Church on earth is never mentioned again after the 3rd chapter. And yet, the people who were getting all excited about this book were the very ones who said they believed in the rapture. Somehow, even after reading the book, they were blinded to the fact that the verse the author used as the basis for his theory is found in Revelation chapter 6. During this time, I had an interesting conversation with a pastor. I finally just asked him if he believed in the pre-tribulation rapture of the church. He said he sure did. I asked him if he believed that the Four Bloods Moons were accurately predicting the return of the Lord. He said he sure did. I then said, well, it looks like you and I both got left behind because Revelation chapter 6 is revealing things that will happen during the Tribulation. That only upset him more. As you can see, the prophesy of that book turned out to be a false prophesy, along with so many others like it. I consider those writers to be false prophets. I don't understand why people continually chase after such fanciful nonsense when the Bible tells us that no man knows the day nor the hour when these events are going to take place. The blood moons we are seeing now are just natural occurrences that have always taken place and will continue to take place. If you reread verses 12-14 of chapter 6, you will see that what is happening in those verses is far from normal or natural. It is a dramatic and drastic event that doesn't even bear any resemblance to what we have seen up to this point in time. But these are the issues that distract us and cause us to miss what is most important. Let me say it one more time. "Leave the timing to God because only He knows." Let's just make sure we are ready whenever Jesus does come back.

Revelation: Chapter 7

Revelation 7:1-4, "(1) And after these things I saw four angels standing on the four corners of the earth, holding the four winds of the earth, that the wind should not blow on the earth, nor on the sea, nor on any tree. (2) And I saw another angel ascending from the east, having the seal of the living God: and he cried with a loud voice to the four angels, to whom it was given to hurt the earth and the sea, (3) Saying, Hurt not the earth, neither the sea, nor the trees, till we have sealed the servants of our God in their foreheads. (4) And I heard the number of them which were sealed: and there were sealed a hundred and forty and four thousand of all the tribes of the children of Israel."

Who are these people? There are some organizations who say that they are the 144,000. Let me mention just one. Jehovah's Witnesses teach that only 144,000 people will go to heaven, and they will come from within their ranks. According to their founder, Charles Taze Russell, the full complement of those who qualified for heaven was completed in 1881. That date was later changed to 1935. All faithful Jehovah's Witnesses not chosen to be among the 144,000 elite that go to heaven as the heavenly class will spend eternity on earth as the earthly class. All other people on the earth will be destroyed at the Battle of Armageddon. This would also include any Jehovah's Witness who has been disfellowshipped. Or one who was unfaithful and has not worked his or her way back into the good graces of the Jehovah Witnesses by the time of the Battle of Armageddon. I used to encounter a lot of this when I did street evangelism, and of course, when the Witnesses came knocking on my door. This is just one example of how Scripture can be distorted. There are many excellent sources to research this, but I still prefer "The Kingdom of the Cults" by Walter Martin.

Some say the 144,000 are symbolic. Those who are into numerology say that twelve is the number of completion. You have twelve sons, you have twelve Apostles, you have twelve gates, you have twelve foundational stones. In this case, you have twelve tribes, and you have twelve-thousand from each of those twelve tribes. Some say that we have lost track of who belongs to which tribe. Even if that were true, God has not lost track of who belongs to which tribe, and it is God who chooses and seals these witnesses. Perhaps this is one of those times when the best thing to do is to just simply take the Bible for what it says instead of trying to make it say what we want it to say. Here's the most important thing to me when I read these verses. The Jewish people have finally come to understand and accept Jesus as the Messiah, and as a result, they are saved. Praise God!

Revelation 7:9-15, "(9) After this I beheld, and, lo, a great multitude, which no man could number, of all nations, and kindreds, and people, and tongues, stood before the throne, and before the Lamb, clothed with white robes, and palms in their hands; (10) And cried with a loud voice, saying, Salvation to our God which sitteth upon the throne, and unto the Lamb. (11) And all the angels stood round about the throne, and about the elders and the four beasts, and fell before the throne on their faces, and worshipped God, (12) Saying, Amen: Blessing, and glory, and wisdom, and thanksgiving, and honour, and power, and might, be unto our God for ever and ever. Amen. (13) And one of the elders answered, saying unto me, What are these which are arrayed in white robes? and whence came they? (14) And I said unto him, Sir, thou knowest. And he said to me, These are they which came out of great tribulation, and have washed their robes, and made them white in the blood of the Lamb. (15) Therefore, are they before the throne of God, and serve Him day and night in His temple: and He that sitteth on the throne shall dwell among them. (16) They shall hunger no more, neither thirst any more; neither shall the sun light on them, nor any heat. (17) For the Lamb which is in the midst of the throne shall feed them and shall lead them unto living fountains of waters: and God shall wipe away all tears from their eyes."

Some say that verse 9 represents the Christians of all ages who have accepted Jesus as their Savior, and that could well be the case. "(9) After this I beheld, and, lo, a great multitude, which no man could number, of all nations, and kindreds, and people, and tongues, stood before the throne, and before the Lamb, clothed with white robes, and palms in their hands." But did you notice what verses 13 & 14 said? "(13) And one of the elders answered, saying unto me, What are these which are arrayed in white robes? and whence came they? (14) And I said unto him, Sir, thou knowest. And he said to me, These are they which came out of great tribulation, and have washed their robes, and made them white in the blood of the Lamb."

There are some who teach that if you miss the rapture that you have no chance of ever being saved. In other words, no one will be saved during the Great Tribulation. It seems obvious to me that this chapter disproves that. I believe that many people will be saved during the Great Tribulation. But, let me add a word of caution. I also believe that those who accept Jesus during this time will most likely die a horrific death. They will have refused the mark of the beast, and the best-case scenario is that they will starve to death. The worst-case scenario is to die a tortured and tormented death. The Great and Terrible Day of the Lord is going to be worse than anything we can conceive. I would also add that the likelihood of people getting saved during the Tribulation begins to diminish the further we progress into the Tribulation. Thank God that His mercy extends to "whosoever will" up until the time when God Himself closes the door.

Verse 17 is an oft-quoted verse and a time that we anxiously await. "For the Lamb which is in the midst of the throne shall feed them and shall lead them unto living fountains of waters: and God shall wipe away all tears from their eyes." No more tears; what a glorious day that will be.

Revelation: Chapter 8

Revelation 8:1, "And when He had opened the seventh seal, there was silence in heaven about the space of half an hour." I have two almost opposing thoughts on these thirty minutes of silence. After I share my thoughts, you can pause and contemplate what you think about it. Chapter 7 has just concluded. Let me remind you that the Bible was not written in chapter and verse. These were added when the Bible was translated so that we could find a particular verse of Scripture. Can you imagine how hard it would be to find anything if we didn't have chapter and verse? In the original text, we simply flow out of what we call chapter 7 into chapter 8. What happened in chapter 7? You have an assembly of people so large that no man can number gathered around the throne, and they are worshipping God and giving Him praise. If loud worship makes you nervous, you will probably be uncomfortable when chapter 7 comes to pass.

Those of us who have lived any length of time know from experience, and the book of Revelation certainly bears this out, that life is not always easy. Not just from what we may suffer physically or emotionally, but from Satan constantly trying to destroy our souls. I've talked to some very good Christian people who have said, "I just want to make it to heaven." And, I feel that way too. I just want to make it to heaven. Well, imagine with me that this verse is capturing that moment when the redeemed of all ages are standing around the throne, praising God for His faithfulness and for keeping His Word. And suddenly, heaven comes to a thirty-minute standstill. People look around, and it dawns on them where they are. They finally made it home!!! Have you ever been in such awe of something that it left you speechless? There is a part of me that believes that this is exactly what is taking place here. I'm home!

The worship that follows in the next few verses gives some validity to this thought. Revelation 8:2-4, "(2) And I saw the seven angels which stood before God; and to them were given seven trumpets. (3) And another angel came and stood at the altar, having a golden censer; and there was given unto him much incense, that he should offer it with the prayers of all saints upon the golden altar which was before the throne. (4) And the smoke of the incense, which came with the prayers of the saints, ascended up before God out of the angel's hand." This is a holy moment in heaven. This is reminiscent of what occurred in the Old Testament when the priest would enter into the Holy Place. There are times when you stand in the Holiness of God that you are so overwhelmed that you are speechless.

But, on the other hand. The Great and Terrible Day of the Lord is just beginning. What is about to happen is almost too awful to contemplate. These thirty-minutes of silence could reflect the shock and awe of what is about to transpire.

Revelation 8:5-13, "(5) And the angel took the censer, and filled it with fire of the altar, and cast it into the earth: and there were voices, and thunderings, and lightnings, and an earthquake. (6) And the seven angels which had the seven trumpets prepared themselves to sound. (7) The first angel sounded, and there followed hail and fire mingled with blood, and they were cast upon the earth: and the third part of trees was burnt up, and all green grass was burnt up. (8) And the second angel sounded, and as it were a great mountain burning with fire was cast into the sea: and the third part of the sea became blood; (9) And the third part of the creatures which were in the sea, and had life, died; and the third part of the ships were destroyed. (10) And the third angel sounded, and there fell a great star from heaven, burning as it were a lamp, and it fell upon the third part of the rivers, and upon the fountains of waters; (11) And the name of the star is called Wormwood: and the third part of the waters became wormwood; and many men died of the waters, because they were made bitter. (12) And the fourth angel sounded, and the third part of the sun was smitten, and the third part of the moon, and the third part of the stars; so as the third part of them was darkened, and the day shone not for a third part of it, and the night likewise. (13) And I beheld, and heard an angel flying through the midst of heaven, saying with a loud voice, Woe, woe, woe, to the inhabiters of the earth by reason of the other voices of the trumpet of the three angels, which are yet to sound!"

In 68 A.D., the Apostle Peter is in Mamertine Prison in Rome. He has been sentenced to death, but Jesus has not returned as Peter thought He would. It's almost like God parted the veil and gave Peter a glimpse of what was going to happen. 2 Peter 3:9-14, "(9) The Lord is not slack concerning His promise, as some men count slackness; but is longsuffering to us-ward, not willing that any should perish, but that all should come to repentance. (10) But the day of the Lord will come as a thief in the night; in the which the heavens shall pass away with a great noise, and the elements shall melt with fervent heat, the earth also and the works that are therein shall be burned up. (11) Seeing then that all these things shall be dissolved, what manner of persons ought ye to be in all holy conversation and godliness, (12) Looking for and hasting unto the coming of the day of God, wherein the heavens being on fire shall be dissolved, and the elements shall melt with fervent heat? (13) Nevertheless we, according to His promise, look for new heavens and a new earth, wherein dwelleth righteousness. (14) Wherefore, beloved, seeing that ye look for such things, be diligent that ye may be found of Him in peace, without spot, and blameless."

The things which are yet to come are shared with us in the Bible so that we will know how to live as we approach the Great and Terrible Day of the Lord. It's doubtful that our minds can fully comprehend just how awful the events of the Great Tribulation are going to be. The destruction continues to escalate and affect more and more people. And, it's all because of sin. The devil is proficient at painting an alluring picture of the pleasures of sin, but he never shows the tragic consequences of the decision to reject God and to disobey His Word.

Revelation: Chapter 9

Revelation 9:1-12, "(1) And the fifth angel sounded, and I saw a star fall from heaven unto the earth: and to him was given the key of the bottomless pit. (2) And he opened the bottomless pit; and there arose a smoke out of the pit, as the smoke of a great furnace; and the sun and the air were darkened by reason of the smoke of the pit. (3) And there came out of the smoke locusts upon the earth: and unto them was given power, as the scorpions of the earth have power. (4) And it was commanded them that they should not hurt the grass of the earth, neither any green thing, neither any tree; but only those men which have not the seal of God in their foreheads. (5) And to them it was given that they should not kill them, but that they should be tormented five months: and their torment was as the torment of a scorpion, when he striketh a man. (6) And in those days shall men seek death and shall not find it; and shall desire to die, and death shall flee from them. (7) And the shapes of the locusts were like unto horses prepared unto battle; and on their heads were as it were crowns like gold, and their faces were as the faces of men. (8) And they had hair as the hair of women, and their teeth were as the teeth of lions. (9) And they had breastplates, as it were breastplates of iron; and the sound of their wings was as the sound of chariots of many horses running to battle. (10) And they had tails like unto scorpions, and there were stings in their tails: and their power was to hurt men five months. (11) And they had a king over them, which is the angel of the bottomless pit, whose name in the Hebrew tongue is Abaddon, but in the Greek tongue hath his name Apollyon. (12) One woe is past; and, behold, there come two woes more hereafter."

Rather than trying to figure out who or what some of these creatures are, this is what sticks out to me in these verses. God's hand of protection is upon those who have His seal upon their forehead. Those who do not have that seal are going to face a time of such torment that they will try to kill themselves, but they cannot. They will seek death, but death will flee from them. Can you imagine the horror of that?

Revelation 9:13-21, "(13) And the sixth angel sounded, and I heard a voice from the four horns of the golden altar which is before God, (14) Saying to the sixth angel which had the trumpet, Loose the four angels which are bound in the great river Euphrates. (15) And the four angels were loosed, which were prepared for an hour, and a day, and a month, and a year, for to slay the third part of men. (16) And the number of the army of the horsemen were two hundred thousand thousand: and I heard the number of them. (17) And thus I saw the horses in the vision, and them that sat on them, having breastplates of fire, and of jacinth, and brimstone:

and the heads of the horses were as the heads of lions; and out of their mouths issued fire and smoke and brimstone. (18) By these three was the third part of men killed, by the fire, and by the smoke, and by the brimstone, which issued out of their mouths. (19) For their power is in their mouth, and in their tails: for their tails were like unto serpents, and had heads, and with them they do hurt. (20) And the rest of the men which were not killed by these plagues yet repented not of the works of their hands, that they should not worship devils, and idols of gold, and silver, and brass, and stone, and of wood: which neither can see, nor hear, nor walk: (21) Neither repented they of their murders, nor of their sorceries, nor of their fornication, nor of their thefts."

I mentioned earlier that the likelihood of people getting saved during the Tribulation begins to diminish the further we progress into the Tribulation, and these two verses seem to express that. Revelation 9:20-21, '(20) And the rest of the men which were not killed by these plagues yet repented not of the works of their hands, that they should not worship devils, and idols of gold, and silver, and brass, and stone, and of wood: which neither can see, nor hear, nor walk: (21) Neither repented they of their murders, nor of their sorceries, nor of their fornication, nor of their thefts."

There comes a time when people reach a point of no return. In the book of Romans, there is a list of sins that eventually have terrifying consequences. Romans 1:28 says, "And even as they did not like to retain God in their knowledge, God gave them over to a reprobate mind, to do those things which are not convenient." We are seeing the fulfillment of this Scripture in our day. There comes a time when people have so rejected God that they are given over to a reprobate mind. Let me caution us and say that only God knows where that point of no return is. There comes a point where instead of people repenting, they get angry at God. We saw that on September 11, 2001. For a few weeks after 9/11, there was a surge in church attendance. But less than a month later, church attendance began to decline, and it hasn't stopped declining since. People got angry at God because of what had happened. That same thing seems to be happening at this point in the book of Revelation. Rather than repenting, the people get angry with God.

Revelation: Chapter 10

Revelation 10:1-11, "(1) And I saw another mighty angel come down from heaven, clothed with a cloud: and a rainbow was upon his head, and his face was as it were the sun, and his feet as pillars of fire: (2) And he had in his hand a little book open: and he set his right foot upon the sea, and his left foot on the earth, (3) And cried with a loud voice, as when a lion roareth: and when he had cried, seven thunders uttered their voices. (4) And when the seven thunders had uttered their voices, I was about to write: and I heard a voice from heaven saying unto me, seal up those things which the seven thunders uttered, and write them not. (5) And the angel which I saw stand upon the sea and upon the earth lifted up his hand to heaven, (6) And sware by him that liveth for ever and ever, who created heaven, and the things that therein are, and the earth, and the things that therein are, and the sea, and the things which are therein, that there should be time no longer: (7) But in the days of the voice of the seventh angel, when he shall begin to sound, the mystery of God should be finished, as he hath declared to his servants the prophets. (8) And the voice which I heard from heaven spake unto me again, and said, Go and take the little book which is open in the hand of the angel which standeth upon the sea and upon the earth. (9) And I went unto the angel, and said unto him, Give me the little book. And he said unto me, take it, and eat it up; and it shall make thy belly bitter, but it shall be in thy mouth sweet as honey. (10) And I took the little book out of the angel's hand and ate it up; and it was in my mouth sweet as honey: and as soon as I had eaten it, my belly was bitter. (11) And he said unto me, thou must prophesy again before many peoples, and nations, and tongues, and kings."

In the early 1970's, a man professed to be the "rainbow prophet." He was one among many who have claimed to be Jesus. A good friend of mine really got caught up in this. I almost never convinced him who this man was professing to be, and that he was just one in a long line of false prophets. The man who claimed to be the "rainbow prophet" is dead and gone now, just like all the other false prophets who preceded him. Jesus warned us of these days.

When God first gave the vision to Daniel, He told Daniel to seal it up. In Revelation, we are seeing an unsealing of that vision. But did you notice verse 4? "And when the seven thunders had uttered their voices, I was about to write: and I heard a voice from heaven saying unto me, seal up those things which the seven thunders uttered, and write them not." With all of the information from both the Old and New Testaments about the last days, there are still parts of it that God doesn't want us to know.

Ezekiel 2:9-10, "(9) And when I looked, behold, an hand was sent unto me; and, lo, a roll of a book was therein; (10) And he spread it before me; and it was written within and without: and there was written therein lamentations, and mourning, and woe."

Ezekiel 3:1-3, "(1) Moreover he said unto me, Son of man, eat that thou findest; eat this roll, and go speak unto the house of Israel. (2) So I opened my mouth, and he caused me to eat that roll. (3) And he said unto me, Son of man, cause thy belly to eat, and fill thy bowels with this roll that I give thee. Then did I eat it; and it was in my mouth as honey for sweetness."

Ezekiel was sent to the children of Israel to preach the God's truth. But Ezekiel 3:7 says that they were "impudent and hardhearted." In other words, they refused to hear. How can a thing be sweet to the mouth but bitter to the belly? In simple terms, I would suggest that to those who love God's Word, it is like honey to the mouth. It is sweet and pleasant. But as both Ezekiel and John saw, when you really see the full consequences of sin, it is not a pleasant thing. John is saying that when he sees and understands what is going on and is not able to reveal it, he is sickened to see what the sinners are going to face. His heart is literally breaking for those who are rejecting salvation. That's a heart of compassion. When I see a supposed Christian gloating over someone who they say is going to get what they deserve one day in hell, I must confess that I cannot understand. It hurts my heart. The Bible plainly tells us that God gets no pleasure in the death of the wicked. Ezekiel 33:11, "As I live, saith the Lord God, I have no pleasure in the death of the wicked; but that the wicked turn from his way and live: turn ye, turn ye from your evil ways; for why will ye die?" If God gets no pleasure in the death of the wicked, why should we? It should trouble us to think about anyone dying lost and spending eternity in a burning lake of fire.

The last verse of chapter 10 must have been encouraging to John. He had been banished to the Isle of Patmos for preaching the Gospel. He may have thought this would be where he would die, that his ministry was over. But God said in verse 11, "Thou must prophesy again before many peoples, and nations, and tongues, and kings." God was telling John that one day he would get off this island. John still had much to do. We know this did happen and that John became a spiritual leader to the seven churches that we see in Revelation, chapters 2 and 3. Even more, the words he wrote down in the book of Revelation have touched countless millions of people.

Revelation: Chapter 11

Revelation 11:1-14, "(1) And there was given me a reed like unto a rod: and the angel stood, saying, Rise, and measure the temple of God, and the altar, and them that worship therein. (2) But the court which is without the temple leave out and measure it not; for it is given unto the Gentiles: and the holy city shall they tread under foot forty and two months. (3) And I will give power unto my two witnesses, and they shall prophesy a thousand two hundred and threescore days, clothed in sackcloth. (4) These are the two olive trees, and the two candlesticks standing before the God of the earth. (5) And if any man will hurt them, fire proceedeth out of their mouth, and devoureth their enemies: and if any man will hurt them, he must in this manner be killed. (6) These have power to shut heaven, that it rain not in the days of their prophecy: and have power over waters to turn them to blood, and to smite the earth with all plagues, as often as they will. (7) And when they shall have finished their testimony, the beast that ascendeth out of the bottomless pit shall make war against them, and shall overcome them, and kill them. (8) And their dead bodies shall lie in the street of the great city, which spiritually is called Sodom and Egypt, where also our Lord was crucified. (9) And they of the people and kindreds and tongues and nations shall see their dead bodies three days and an half, and shall not suffer their dead bodies to be put in graves. (10) And they that dwell upon the earth shall rejoice over them, and make merry, and shall send gifts one to another; because these two prophets tormented them that dwelt on the earth. (11) And after three days and an half the spirit of life from God entered into them, and they stood upon their feet; and great fear fell upon them which saw them. (12) And they heard a great voice from heaven saying unto them, Come up hither. And they ascended up to heaven in a cloud; and their enemies beheld them. (13) And the same hour was there a great earthquake, and the tenth part of the city fell, and in the earthquake were slain of men seven thousand: and the remnant were affrighted, and gave glory to the God of heaven. (14) The second woe is past; and, behold, the third woe cometh quickly."

Who are these two witnesses of Revelation 11:3? We are introduced to them in the Old Testament in the book of Zechariah. Zechariah 4:1-5 and 11-14; "(1) And the angel that talked with me came again, and waked me, as a man that is wakened out of his sleep. (2) And said unto me, What seest thou? And I said, I have looked, and behold a candlestick all of gold, with a bowl upon the top of it, and his seven lamps thereon, and seven pipes to the seven lamps, which are upon the top thereof: (3) And two olive trees by it, one upon the right side of the bowl, and the other upon the left side thereof. (4) So I answered and spake to the angel that talked with me, saying, What are these, my lord? (5) Then the angel that talked with me answered and said unto me, Knowest thou not what these be? And I said, No, my lord."

Drop down to verse 11. "(11) Then answered I, and said unto him, What are these two olive trees upon the right side of the candlestick and upon the left side thereof? (12) And I answered again, and said unto him, What be these two olive branches which through the two golden pipes empty the golden oil out of themselves? (13) And he answered me and said, Knowest thou not what these be? And I said, No, my lord. (14) Then said he, These are the two anointed ones, that stand by the Lord of the whole earth."

There are two opinions as to who these witnesses are. Some say they are Enoch and Elijah. The main reason for this belief is because of the Scripture in Hebrews 9:27 which says, "And as it is appointed unto men once to die, but after this the judgment." Hebrews 11:5 says, "By faith Enoch was translated that he should not see death; and was not found, because God had translated him: for before his translation he had this testimony, that he pleased God." So, Enoch did not die. While the Bible does not say that Elijah did not die, it seems to be implied because we see him taken to heaven in a fiery chariot. So, some conclude that they must be the two witnesses since everybody has to die.

Some say it was Moses and Elijah because they are the two who appeared with Jesus on the Mount of Transfiguration. They represent the Law and the Prophets. Matthew 17:1-3, "(1) And after six days Jesus taketh Peter, James, and John his brother, and bringeth them up into an high mountain apart, (2) And was transfigured before them: and His face did shine as the sun, and His raiment was white as the light. (3) And, behold, there appeared unto them Moses and Elias talking with Him."

Elijah is the only one who shows up in both suppositions, primarily for two reasons. Malachi 4:5, "Behold, I will send you Elijah the prophet before the coming of the great and dreadful day of the Lord." The scripture in Malachi is clearly talking about the great and dreadful day of the Lord. Some think that this was a reference to a reincarnated Elijah as John the Baptist. But if Elijah never died, he couldn't be reincarnated as a living person. And, such a theory would have the Bible validating reincarnation, which it does not. Does that mean that Elijah came back down to earth to live as John the Baptist, and then after John was beheaded, he showed back up on the Mount of Transfiguration as Elijah? Don't you think that gets a wee bit confusing? John the Baptist was asked one day if he was Elijah. He responded in John 1:21, "And they asked him, What then? Art thou Elias? And he saith, I am not."

The confusion on this issue comes from a statement that Jesus made to His disciples one day. Matthew 11:14, "And if ye will receive it, this is Elias, which was for to come." In this chapter, John the Baptist has been thrown into prison. He sends two of his followers to Jesus to ask Him if He, Jesus, was the Messiah they had been waiting for. Even though John the Baptist had been bolder than most, he was now facing a time of questioning. "Are you the One I preached about?" Jesus didn't tell the disciples of John the Baptist point blank that He was that One of whom John preached, but He told them to go tell John what He was doing. This was a fulfillment of the Scriptures that pointed to the Messiah, and John the Baptist clearly understood that Jesus was saying, "Yes, I am he."

Jesus then proceeds to give John the Baptist the greatest compliment that anyone has ever been given. In Luke 7:28, Jesus said that "no one among those born of women is greater than John." Sometimes a compliment can be judged by the person who says it, and Jesus is the one who said this. In Matthew chapter 11, Jesus is reminding His disciples of the Law and the Prophets and what they said about Him. These disciples knew about the prophecy of Malachi. That's why this question came up on a couple of occasions. I'm sure they also knew the exact wording of Malachi 4: 5, "Behold, I will send you Elijah the prophet before the coming of the great and dreadful day of the Lord." Was the occasion when Jesus was speaking to His disciples the Great and Terrible Day of the Lord referred to in Revelation? The answer is "no". But just like Elijah will be the messenger or the forerunner of that future event, so was John the Baptist the messenger or the forerunner of the earthly ministry of Jesus. Jesus asked His disciples if they could accept this. They must have accepted it because the question was never asked again.

A clear understanding of this subject is found in Luke 1:13-17, "(13) But the angel said unto him, Fear not, Zacharias: for thy prayer is heard; and thy wife Elisabeth shall bear thee a son, and thou shalt call his name John. (14) And thou shalt have joy and gladness; and many shall rejoice at his birth. (15) For he shall be great in the sight of the Lord and shall drink neither wine nor strong drink; and he shall be filled with the Holy Ghost, even from his mother's womb. (16) And many of the children of Israel shall he turn to the Lord their God. (17) And he shall go before Him in the spirit and power of Elias, to turn the hearts of the fathers to the children, and the disobedient to the wisdom of the just; to make ready a people prepared for the Lord."

When the angel appeared to Zacharias announcing the birth of John, he plainly said in verse 17, "And he shall go before Him (Jesus) in the spirit and power of Elias, to turn the hearts of the fathers to the children, and the disobedient to the wisdom of the just; to make ready a people prepared for the Lord." A distinction has to be made between the two men and the two events.

The second reason that some say that Elijah will be one of the witnesses of Revelation 10:3 is because just like Elijah prayed and the heavens were shut up for three and a half years in the Old Testament, that will happen again in the Great Tribulation. James 5:17, "Elijah was a man subject to like passions as we are, and he prayed earnestly that it might not rain: and it rained not on the earth by the space of three years and six months." Revelation 11:6, "These have power to shut heaven, that it rain not in the days of their prophecy." Since Revelation chapter 11 clearly states that the length of these two witness's prophecies is three and a half years, some see this as another proof that God will use Elijah in this capacity again.

Some say the second witness is Moses instead of Enoch because the plagues such as turning the water into blood were a part of Moses ministry, coupled with the fact that it was clearly Moses and Elijah on the Mount of Transfiguration. Who will be the two witnesses of Revelation chapter 11? Let's all look down from heaven one day and see if anybody was right

Here is the important part of these verses. Their ministry will last for three and a half years, and during that time the two witnesses are untouchable. They are divinely protected by God. But when their ministry is completed, they are killed. As an added insult, their dead bodies are left in the streets for the whole world to see, and it causes great rejoicing. With the technology we have today, this is possible. Leaving their bodies in the street violates every Jewish law, but the Antichrist doesn't care. He is just overjoyed to be rid of them, and whatever humiliation he can heap upon them, he will gladly do. After three and a half days, God intervenes, and the two witnesses are raised from the dead and ascend into heaven. The worlds rejoicing turns into terror. There were no cameras to capture the sight when Jesus ascended into heaven 2,000 years ago, but the world will see this ascension.

Revelation 11:15-19, "(15) And the seventh angel sounded; and there were great voices in heaven, saying, the kingdoms of this world are become the kingdoms of our Lord, and of His Christ; and He shall reign for ever and ever. (16) And the four and twenty elders, which sat before God on their seats, fell upon their faces, and worshipped God, (17) Saying, we give Thee thanks, O Lord God Almighty, which art, and wast, and art to come; because Thou hast taken to Thee Thy great power, and hast reigned. (18) And the nations were angry, and Thy wrath is come, and the time of the dead, that they should be judged, and that Thou shouldest give reward unto Thy servants the prophets, and to the saints, and them that fear Thy name, small and great; and shouldest destroy them which destroy the earth. (19) And the temple of God was opened in heaven, and there was seen in His Temple the ark of His testament: and there were lightnings, and voices, and thunderings, and an earthquake, and great hail."

As the events of the Great Tribulation continue, an interesting tidbit of information is given to us. People have been looking for the Ark of the Covenant for hundreds of years. Verse 19 gives us the exact location. It is in heaven. It is not in Israel, Egypt or any other place on earth. At some point God just took it on to heaven. I guess Hollywood missed that part!

Revelation: Chapter 12

Revelation 12:1-17, "(1) And there appeared a great wonder in heaven; a woman clothed with the sun, and the moon under her feet, and upon her head a crown of twelve stars: (2) And she being with child cried, travailing in birth, and pained to be delivered. (3) And there appeared another wonder in heaven; and behold a great red dragon, having seven heads and ten horns, and seven crowns upon his heads. (4) And his tail drew the third part of the stars of heaven and did cast them to the earth: and the dragon stood before the woman which was ready to be delivered, for to devour her child as soon as it was born. (5) And she brought forth a man child, who was to rule all nations with a rod of iron: and her child was caught up unto God, and to his throne. (6) And the woman fled into the wilderness, where she hath a place prepared of God, that they should feed her there a thousand two hundred and threescore days. (7) And there was war in heaven: Michael and his angels fought against the dragon; and the dragon fought and his angels, (8) And prevailed not; neither was their place found any more in heaven. (9) And the great dragon was cast out, that old serpent, called the Devil, and Satan, which deceiveth the whole world: he was cast out into the earth, and his angels were cast out with him. (10) And I heard a loud voice saying in heaven, Now is come salvation, and strength, and the kingdom of our God, and the power of his Christ: for the accuser of our brethren is cast down, which accused them before our God day and night. (11) And they overcame him by the blood of the Lamb, and by the word of their testimony; and they loved not their lives unto the death. (12) Therefore rejoice, ye heavens, and ye that dwell in them. Woe to the inhabiters of the earth and of the sea! for the devil is come down unto you, having great wrath, because he knoweth that he hath but a short time. (13) And when the dragon saw that he was cast unto the earth, he persecuted the woman which brought forth the man child. (14) And to the woman were given two wings of a great eagle, that she might fly into the wilderness, into her place, where she is nourished for a time, and times, and half a time, from the face of the serpent. (15) And the serpent cast out of his mouth water as a flood after the woman, that he might cause her to be carried away of the flood. (16) And the earth helped the woman, and the earth opened her mouth, and swallowed up the flood which the dragon cast out of his mouth. (17) And the dragon was wroth with the woman and went to make war with the remnant of her seed, which keep the commandments of God, and have the testimony of Jesus Christ."

Revelation chapter 12 is a parenthetical chapter of sorts, at least in part. A portion of this chapter interrupts the current story to tell us about something else. The story it tells predates the book of Genesis. Jesus speaks of this in Luke 10:17-18. Jesus had sent out 70 of His disciples to preach the good news that the Kingdom of God is nigh and to heal the sick. They come back to Jesus with a report of a successful ministry trip. "(17) And the seventy returned again with joy, saying, Lord, even the devils are subject unto us through thy name. (18) And He said unto them, I beheld Satan as lightning fall from heaven."

On the one hand, Jesus seems to have completely ignored what they were saying with His response. To what was Jesus referring? In Isaiah chapter 14:12-15, we read, "(12) How art thou fallen from heaven, O Lucifer, son of the morning! how art thou cut down to the ground, which didst weaken the nations! (13) For thou hast said in thine heart, I will ascend into heaven, I will exalt my throne above the stars of God: I will sit also upon the mount of the congregation, in the sides of the north: (14) I will ascend above the heights of the clouds; I will be like the most High. (15) Yet thou shalt be brought down to hell, to the sides of the pit." This is the event that Jesus was talking about.

The prophet Ezekiel was among the second group of captives who were taken into Babylonian captivity in 597 B.C. So, he is writing these words from Babylon. Ezekiel 28:11-19, "(11) Moreover the word of the Lord came unto me, saying, (12) Son of man, take up a lamentation upon the king of Tyrus, and say unto him, Thus saith the Lord God; Thou sealest up the sum, full of wisdom, and perfect in beauty. (13) Thou hast been in Eden the garden of God; every precious stone was thy covering, the sardius, topaz, and the diamond, the beryl, the onyx, and the jasper, the sapphire, the emerald, and the carbuncle, and gold: the workmanship of thy tabrets and of thy pipes was prepared in thee in the day that thou wast created. (14) Thou art the anointed cherub that covereth; and I have set thee so: thou wast upon the holy mountain of God; thou hast walked up and down in the midst of the stones of fire. (15) Thou wast perfect in thy ways from the day that thou wast created, till iniquity was found in thee. (16) By the multitude of thy merchandise they have filled the midst of thee with violence, and thou hast sinned: therefore, I will cast thee as profane out of the mountain of God: and I will destroy thee, O covering cherub, from the midst of the stones of fire. (17) Thine heart was lifted up because of thy beauty, thou hast corrupted thy wisdom by reason of thy brightness: I will cast thee to the ground, I will lay thee before kings, that they may behold thee. (18) Thou hast defiled thy sanctuaries by the multitude of thine iniquities, by the iniquity of thy traffick; therefore, will I bring forth a fire from the midst of thee, it shall devour thee, and I will bring thee to ashes upon the earth in the sight of all them that behold thee. (19) All they that know thee among the people shall be astonished at thee: thou shalt be a terror, and never shalt thou be any more."

Angels are created beings, and it is obvious that they had a free will. There was one angel, Lucifer, who chose to rebel against God. He was at one time an anointed angel. He is believed to have been one of the three greatest angels with Michael and Gabriel being the other two. He convinced a third of the angels in heaven, who he seems to have had authority over, to follow him in his attempted overthrow of God. There was a war in heaven because Lucifer wanted to be God. Satan (Lucifer) was cast out of heaven, but the conflict still continues till today. The Bible lets us know that there is an end to this war coming at some point in the future, and the book of Revelation gives us an outline as to how this will happen.

Why in the midst of the joyous celebration of Luke's gospel did Jesus respond to His disciples this way? While they certainly had much to be thankful for as a result of their recent missionary endeavor, it would seem they were a little too boastful or proud. When Jesus saw their pride, it reminded Him of an incident that happened in the dateless past. It was pride that caused Satan to be cast out of heaven, and it is pride that has caused many a good person to go wrong. Proverbs 16:18 says, "Pride goeth before destruction, and an haughty spirit before a fall." Jesus was telling His disciples to be careful that pride doesn't cause them to fall. Jesus then added these words, Luke 10:19-20, "(19) Behold, I give unto you power to tread on serpents and scorpions, and over all the power of the enemy: and nothing shall by any means hurt you. (20) Notwithstanding in this rejoice not, that the spirits are subject unto you; but rather rejoice, because your names are written in heaven." Jesus reminds us that regardless of whatever measure of success we may have in ministry, the greatest thing for us to celebrate is that our names are written in the Lamb's Book of Life. That is cause for celebrating and rejoicing.

Let me call your attention to Revelation 12:11, "And they overcame him by the blood of the Lamb, and by the word of their testimony." This is a Scripture that I share as often as I can with new converts. In the context of chapter 12, it is obviously dealing with the events of the Tribulation, but there is a principle here that transcends any one moment in time. It tells us how to live a victorious Christian life. The first part says that we are made overcomers by the blood of the Lamb. That's the part that we cannot do for ourselves. Jesus shed His blood for us and made salvation possible for "whosoever will". But the second half of that verse is what we can do. "We are made overcomers by the word of our testimony." We each have a story to tell of how God saved and delivered us. And the more we tell it, the stronger our faith grows. How many times in the Bible do we see this principle? There is a part that only God can do, but then God expects us to do our part. Salvation is by grace through faith, but our works must follow.

Revelation: Chapter 13

Revelation 13:1-18, "(1) And I stood upon the sand of the sea, and saw a beast rise up out of the sea, having seven heads and ten horns, and upon his horns ten crowns, and upon his heads the name of blasphemy. (2) And the beast which I saw was like unto a leopard, and his feet were as the feet of a bear, and his mouth as the mouth of a lion: and the dragon gave him his power, and his seat, and great authority. (3) And I saw one of his heads as it were wounded to death; and his deadly wound was healed: and all the world wondered after the beast. (4) And they worshipped the dragon which gave power unto the beast: and they worshipped the beast, saying, Who is like unto the beast? who is able to make war with him? (5) And there was given unto him a mouth speaking great things and blasphemies; and power was given unto him to continue forty and two months. (6) And he opened his mouth in blasphemy against God, to blaspheme his name, and his tabernacle, and them that dwell in heaven. (7) And it was given unto him to make war with the saints, and to overcome them: and power was given him over all kindreds, and tongues, and nations. (8) And all that dwell upon the earth shall worship him, whose names are not written in the book of life of the Lamb slain from the foundation of the world. (9) If any man have an ear, let him hear. (10) He that leadeth into captivity shall go into captivity: he that killeth with the sword must be killed with the sword. Here is the patience and the faith of the saints. (11) And I beheld another beast coming up out of the earth; and he had two horns like a lamb, and he spake as a dragon. (12) And he exerciseth all the power of the first beast before him, and causeth the earth and them which dwell therein to worship the first beast, whose deadly wound was healed. (13) And he doeth great wonders, so that he maketh fire come down from heaven on the earth in the sight of men, (14) And deceiveth them that dwell on the earth by the means of those miracles which he had power to do in the sight of the beast; saying to them that dwell on the earth, that they should make an image to the beast, which had the wound by a sword, and did live. (15) And he had power to give life unto the image of the beast, that the image of the beast should both speak, and cause that as many as would not worship the image of the beast should be killed. (16) And he causeth all, both small and great, rich and poor, free and bond, to receive a mark in their right hand, or in their foreheads: (17) And that no man might buy or sell, save he that had the mark, or the name of the beast, or the number of his name. (18) Here is wisdom. Let him that hath understanding count the number of the beast: for it is the number of a man; and his number is Six hundred threescore and six."

We have just been introduced to the unholy trinity: The dragon, who is Satan; the beast, who is the Antichrist; and the False Prophet. We are also brought face to face with the Mark of the Beast. Although Satan has a long history, the Antichrist and the False Prophet are essentially contained within the seven-year period of the Tribulation. The Antichrist is the one who is able to bring peace. A covenant is established that is broken after 3 ½ years, and the reason it's broken is because the Antichrist reveals his true intent when he sets up an image of himself in the Temple and proclaims himself to be God. It is the "abomination of desolation" that is spoken of by Jesus, by Daniel, and by others. In 2 Thessalonians 2:1-4, the Apostle Paul addressed this when he said, "(1) Now we beseech you, brethren, by the coming of our Lord Jesus Christ, and by our gathering together unto Him, (2) That ye be not soon shaken in mind, or be troubled, neither by spirit, nor by word, nor by letter as from us, as that the day of Christ is at hand. (3) Let no man deceive you by any means: for that day shall not come, except there come a falling away first, and that man of sin be revealed, the son of perdition; (4) Who opposeth and exalteth himself above all that is called God, or that is worshipped; so that he as God sitteth in the temple of God, shewing himself that he is God."

People have been speculating on who the Antichrist is for years. Nero was probably the first candidate, and he certainly was insane. Napoleon was thought to be the Antichrist also. For those living during World War II, Hitler was certainly a likely candidate. Then, you had people doing crazy things like saying the Antichrist was John F. Kennedy, Henry Kissinger and a long list of people whose numerical value of their names added up to 666. Just about every American President has been thought to be the Antichrist. When President Kennedy was shot, some people went absolutely crazy saying that this was Scripture being fulfilled. They anxiously waited for the False Prophet to heal him of his deadly wound to the head and raise him from the dead. I know this to be true because I lived through that time in history. The one who has been on the list the most consistently is the Pope; it doesn't matter which one, just the Pope.

We see the dragon (Satan) giving his authority to the beast, (the Antichrist) who sets himself up as God. Daniel 7:13-28, "(13) I saw in the night visions, and, behold, one like the Son of man came with the clouds of heaven, and came to the Ancient of days, and they brought Him near before Him. (14) And there was given Him dominion, and glory, and a kingdom, that all people, nations, and languages, should serve Him: His dominion is an everlasting dominion, which shall not pass away, and His kingdom that which shall not be destroyed. (15) I Daniel was grieved in my spirit in the midst of my body, and the visions of my head troubled me. (16)

I came near unto one of them that stood by, and asked him the truth of all this. So he told me, and made me know the interpretation of the things. (17) These great beasts, which are four, are four kings, which shall arise out of the earth. (18) But the saints of the most High shall take the kingdom, and possess the kingdom forever, even for ever and ever. (19) Then I would know the truth of the fourth beast, which was diverse from all the others, exceeding dreadful, whose teeth were of iron, and his nails of brass; which devoured, brake in pieces, and stamped the residue with his feet; (20) And of the ten horns that were in his head, and of the other which came up, and before whom three fell; even of that horn that had eyes, and a mouth that spake very great things, whose look was more stout than his fellows. (21) I beheld, and the same horn made war with the saints, and prevailed against them; (22) Until the Ancient of days came, and judgment was given to the saints of the most High; and the time came that the saints possessed the kingdom. (23) Thus he said, The fourth beast shall be the fourth kingdom upon earth, which shall be diverse from all kingdoms, and shall devour the whole earth, and shall tread it down, and break it in pieces. (24) And the ten horns out of this kingdom are ten kings that shall arise: and another shall rise after them; and he shall be diverse from the first, and he shall subdue three kings. (25) And he shall speak great words against the most High and shall wear out the saints of the most High, and think to change times and laws: and they shall be given into his hand until a time and times and the dividing of time. (26) But the judgment shall sit, and they shall take away his dominion, to consume and to destroy it unto the end. (27) And the kingdom and dominion, and the greatness of the kingdom under the whole heaven, shall be given to the people of the saints of the most High, whose kingdom is an everlasting kingdom, and all dominions shall serve and obey him. (28) Hitherto is the end of the matter."

The rebellion that caused Satan, also known as Lucifer. to be cast out of heaven continues to play itself out. Lucifer wanted to be God; he still does. Everything that is unfolding right now and will continue into the Tribulation is simply Satan doing everything he can to overthrow God and be God himself. It is vividly acted out in the Tribulation when you have the unholy trinity of Satan as God, the Antichrist as the Christ, and the False Prophet as the Holy Ghost.

The deadly head wound that I mentioned earlier is not symbolic. It is literal. The Antichrist will be killed and then brought back to life, just like Jesus was killed and came back to life. The devil is trying to copy what God has done. Just as we worship God the Father through Jesus the Son, Satan sets himself up as the ultimate person of worship in chapter 13, and it comes through the worship of the Antichrist. It is an imitation of the true God.

What about the False Prophet? He's just another imitation of the real thing. Revelation 13:11-13, "(11) And I beheld another beast coming up out of the earth; and he had two horns like a lamb, and he spake as a dragon. (12) And he exerciseth all the power of the first beast before him, and causeth the earth and them which dwell therein to worship the first beast, whose deadly wound was healed. (13) And he doeth great wonders, so that he maketh fire come down from heaven on the earth in the sight of men." Just as the Holy Ghost does not speak of Himself or point people to Himself but rather directs them to Jesus, the False Prophet points people to the Antichrist. They do not worship the False Prophet. They worship the Antichrist. You can also see more of the imitation of the real when it says that the False Prophet can call fire down from heaven. What happened in Acts chapter 2 on the Day of Pentecost when the Holy Ghost came down? Acts 2:3, "There appeared unto them cloven tongues of fire."

Revelation: Chapter 14

Revelation 14:1-20, "(1) And I looked, and, lo, a Lamb stood on the mount Sion, and with Him an hundred forty and four thousand, having his Father's name written in their foreheads. (2) And I heard a voice from heaven, as the voice of many waters, and as the voice of a great thunder: and I heard the voice of harpers harping with their harps: (3) And they sung as it were a new song before the throne, and before the four beasts, and the elders: and no man could learn that song but the hundred and forty and four thousand, which were redeemed from the earth. (4) These are they which were not defiled with women; for they are virgins. These are they which follow the Lamb whithersoever he goeth. These were redeemed from among men, being the firstfruits unto God and to the Lamb. (5) And in their mouth was found no guile: for they are without fault before the throne of God. (6) And I saw another angel fly in the midst of heaven, having the everlasting gospel to preach unto them that dwell on the earth, and to every nation, and kindred, and tongue, and people, (7) Saying with a loud voice, Fear God, and give glory to Him; for the hour of His judgment is come: and worship Him that made heaven, and earth, and the sea, and the fountains of waters. (8) And there followed another angel, saying, Babylon is fallen, is fallen, that great city, because she made all nations drink of the wine of the wrath of her fornication. (9) And the third angel followed them, saying with a loud voice, If any man worship the beast and his image, and receive his mark in his forehead, or in his hand, (10) The same shall drink of the wine of the wrath of God, which is poured out without mixture into the cup of his indignation; and he shall be tormented with fire and brimstone in the presence of the holy angels, and in the presence of the Lamb: (11) And the smoke of their torment ascendeth up for ever and ever: and they have no rest day nor night, who worship the beast and his image, and whosoever receiveth the mark of his name. (12) Here is the patience of the saints: here are they that keep the commandments of God, and the faith of Jesus. (13) And I heard a voice from heaven saying unto me, Write, Blessed are the dead which die in the Lord from henceforth: Yea, saith the Spirit, that they may rest from their labours; and their works do follow them. (14) And I looked, and behold a white cloud, and upon the cloud one sat like unto the Son of man, having on His head a golden crown, and in His hand a sharp sickle. (15) And another angel came out of the temple, crying with a loud voice to Him that sat on the cloud, Thrust in thy sickle, and reap: for the time is come for thee to reap; for the harvest of the earth is ripe. (16) And He that sat on the cloud thrust in his sickle on the earth; and the earth was reaped. (17) And another angel came out of the temple which is in heaven, he also having a sharp sickle. (18) And another angel came out from the altar, which had power over fire; and cried with a loud cry to him that had the sharp sickle, saying, Thrust in thy sharp sickle, and gather the clusters of the vine of the earth; for her grapes are fully ripe. (19) And the angel thrust in his sickle into the earth, and gathered the vine of the earth, and cast it into the great winepress of the wrath of God. (20) And the winepress was trodden without the city, and blood came out of the winepress, even unto the horse bridles, by the space of a thousand and six hundred furlongs."

This chapter begins with the beautiful image of Jesus standing on the top of Mt. Zion with the 144,000 specially called messengers around Him. The mention of how the Father's name is written upon their foreheads is intended to show that their witness is bold. They are not ashamed of the Gospel of Jesus Christ. The statement that they are virgins could be literal, spiritual, or both. Given what was written in chapter 13, perhaps the best understanding of this would be to say that they had kept themselves clean from the abominations of the Antichrist generation. Their hearts were pure before God.

Three angels are seen flying through the heavens, and they each have a message. The first angel is preaching the Gospel. Why would there be a reason to preach the Gospel unless there was an opportunity to accept it? Matthew 24:14. "And this

Gospel of the kingdom shall be preached in all the world for a witness unto all nations; and then shall the end come." If there should happen to be any place that has not heard the Gospel at this point in time, this angel flying through the heavens will ensure that Matthew 24:14 is fulfilled. And then shall the end come. This angel also carries a message of warning that the hour of judgement is at hand and that man should worship the One who created all things.

The second angel informs the world that Babylon has fallen. We will see later in Revelation that this causes great sorrow from those living in sin but great rejoicing from the saints of God. The preaching of the true Gospel will always destroy false religion. Wickedness will not prevail, and sin will not win.

The third angel warns of the terrible consequences of receiving the Mark of the Beast and how those who receive it will be tormented in the lake of fire. Eventually, all who have rejected Christ will be sentenced there, along with Satan, the Antichrist and the False Prophet.

Verse 13 says, "Blessed are the dead which die in the Lord, and their works do follow after them." This verse has been used many times at the funeral of a godly individual who leaves behind a great legacy. Although they have completed their earthly race, the impact of their life continues to touch the generations who follow after them. Each of us knows someone who has impacted our life not only while they were living, but even after they died. This reminds us that God can continue to use the testimony we leave behind. It should encourage us to live in such a manner that these words can be said in a favorable manner about us.

The sickle and the harvest that are mentioned in verse 16 speak about the carnage from the Battle of Armageddon. We see that not only does the Son of Man thrust in a sickle, but multiple angels do as well. The result is that blood will flow up to the bridle of a horse and for a distance of almost 200 miles.

Revelation: Chapter 15

Revelation 15:1-8, "(1) And I saw another sign in heaven, great and marvelous, seven angels having the seven last plagues; for in them is filled up the wrath of God. (2) And I saw as it were a sea of glass mingled with fire: and them that had gotten the victory over the beast, and over his image, and over his mark, and over the number of his name, stand on the sea of glass, having the harps of God. (3) And they sing the song of Moses the servant of God, and the song of the Lamb, saying, Great and marvelous are Thy works, Lord God Almighty; just and true are Thy ways, Thou King of saints. (4) Who shall not fear Thee, O Lord, and glorify Thy name? for Thou only art holy: for all nations shall come and worship before Thee; for Thy judgments are made manifest. (5) And after that I looked, and, behold, the temple of the tabernacle of the testimony in heaven was opened: (6) And the seven angels came out of the temple, having the seven plagues, clothed in pure and white linen, and having their breasts girded with golden girdles. (7) And one of the four beasts gave unto the seven angels seven golden vials full of the wrath of God, who liveth for ever and ever. (8) And the temple was filled with smoke from the glory of God, and from His power; and no man was able to enter into the temple, till the seven plagues of the seven angels were fulfilled."

Chapter 15 is the shortest chapter in the book of Revelation. It gives us a bit of a reprieve from everything that is happening on the earth, and it gives us a glimpse of what is happening in heaven. We see in verse 1 that while we have not reached the conclusion of the "things which are yet to be," we are drawing closer to the final defeat of Satan and the Antichrist. There are seven plagues which remain, but they contain the fulness of the wrath of God.

Verse 2 is another Scripture that proves people will be saved during the Great Tribulation. We see that those who overcame the Antichrist and the mark of the beast are now in the presence of God. In verses 3 and 4, they burst forth with a song of praise. A comparison is drawn between the song of Moses and the song of the Lamb. A simple comparison of the two reveals that they are both songs of deliverance, songs of triumph, and songs of salvation. Those who were in bondage have been set free. This would certainly be the case with the song that Moses sang in Exodus 15:1-2, "(1) Then sang Moses and the children of Israel this song unto the Lord, and spake, saying, I will sing unto the Lord, for He hath triumphed gloriously: the horse and his rider hath He thrown into the sea. (2) The Lord is my strength and song, and He is become my salvation: He is my God, and I will prepare Him an habitation; my father's God, and I will exalt Him." Because of Jesus, our enemies are defeated, and He has set us free.

However, a second song of Moses is recorded in Deuteronomy chapters 31 and 32. The first song occurred when the children of Israel began their journey to the Promised Land. The second song comes forty-years later, shortly before Moses dies. The children of Israel finally enter a land flowing with milk and honey, the place they had been longing for. Moses exhorts them to remember the faithfulness of God and how God has preserved them and sustained them since the day of their deliverance. But Moses also warns them of the dangers that will befall them in the coming days. Looking back upon this second song, we know from a historical perspective that the children of Israel did indeed turn away from God and begin to serve other gods. It led to the wrath of God being poured out upon them. In that respect, the book of Revelation connects these two songs for they both deal with the wrath and judgment of God.

Both songs are relevant. The one about deliverance and victory as well as the song of wrath and judgement. Remember, Revelation is the completion of everything that God has been doing since the dawn of creation. It all finds its ultimate fulfillment on the final pages of the Bible.

Verse 8 says, "And the temple was filled with smoke from the glory of God, and from His power; and no man was able to enter into the temple." You can't help but be carried back to two incidents in the Old Testament. Exodus chapter 40, verse 35; "And Moses was not able to enter into the tent of the congregation, because the cloud abode thereon, and the glory of the Lord filled the tabernacle." The day they dedicated the wilderness tabernacle, the "Shekinah" glory of God was so powerful that Moses could not enter.

A similar thing occurred on the day that Solomon dedicated the temple in Jerusalem. 1 Kings 8: 10-11, "(10) And it came to pass, when the priests were come out of the holy place, that the cloud filled the house of the Lord, (11) So that the priests could not stand to minister because of the cloud: for the glory of the Lord had filled the house of the Lord." The glory of God descended in such a powerful way that the priests could not even stand. They had to bow in the presence of a Holy God. We see that happening again in the book of Revelation.

Yes, chapter 15 is a bit of a reprieve, but it also lets us know that heaven is getting ready for the final showdown. The Great and Terrible Day of the Lord is not over yet.

Revelation: Chapter 16

Revelation 16:1-9, "(1) And I heard a great voice out of the temple saying to the seven angels, Go your ways, and pour out the vials of the wrath of God upon the earth. (2) And the first went, and poured out his vial upon the earth; and there fell a noisome and grievous sore upon the men which had the mark of the beast, and upon them which worshipped his image. (3) And the second angel poured out his vial upon the sea; and it became as the blood of a dead man: and every living soul died in the sea. (4) And the third angel poured out his vial upon the rivers and fountains of waters; and they became blood. (5) And I heard the angel of the waters say, Thou art righteous, O Lord, which art, and wast, and shalt be, because thou hast judged thus. (6) For they have shed the blood of saints and prophets, and thou hast given them blood to drink; for they are worthy. (7) And I heard another out of the altar say, Even so, Lord God Almighty, true and righteous are thy judgments. (8) And the fourth angel poured out his vial upon the sun; and power was given unto him to scorch men with fire. (9) And men were scorched with great heat, and blasphemed the name of God, which hath power over these plagues: and they repented not to give Him glory."

I have mentioned previously how people can reach a point where rather than repent, they get angry with God. And, I illustrated that truth with the tragic events of September 11, 2001. Here is Scriptural proof that people can reach this sad and unfortunate condition of being angry with God. Although they have had numerous opportunities to repent, they continue to blaspheme the name of God and refuse to repent.

Revelation 16:10-21, "(10) And the fifth angel poured out his vial upon the seat of the beast; and his kingdom was full of darkness; and they gnawed their tongues for pain, (11) And blasphemed the God of heaven because of their pains and their sores and repented not of their deeds. (12) And the sixth angel poured out his vial upon the great river Euphrates; and the water thereof was dried up, that the way of the kings of the east might be prepared. (13) And I saw three unclean spirits like frogs come out of the mouth of the dragon, and out of the mouth of the beast, and out of the mouth of the false prophet. (14) For they are the spirits of devils, working miracles, which go forth unto the kings of the earth and of the whole world, to gather them to the battle of that great day of God Almighty. (15) Behold, I come as a thief. Blessed is he that watcheth, and keepeth his garments, lest he walk naked, and they see his shame. (16) And he gathered them together into a place called in the Hebrew tongue Armageddon. (17) And the seventh angel poured out his vial into the air; and there came a great voice out of the temple of heaven, from the throne, saying, It is done. (18) And there were voices, and thunders, and lightnings; and there was a great earthquake, such as was not since men were upon the earth, so mighty an earthquake, and so great. (19) And the great city was divided into three parts, and the cities of the nations fell: and great Babylon came in remembrance before God, to give unto her the cup of the wine of the fierceness of His wrath. (20) And every island fled away, and the mountains were not found. (21) And there fell upon men a great hail out of heaven, every stone about the weight of a talent: and men blasphemed God because of the plague of the hail; for the plague thereof was exceeding great."

In verse 11, for the second time in this chapter, we see hatred and anger expressed toward God. They still refuse to repent. The events of the Great Tribulation are reaching a climax. If the first fifteen chapters of Revelation did not convince you that you do not want to be on earth during this time, then surely chapter 16 does.

I have been blessed on numerous occasions to stand in ruins of the ancient city of Megiddo in Israel. It overlooks a beautiful valley, and it is said that more wars have been fought there than any other place on earth. The earliest accounts of a major war that took place at Megiddo were in the 15th century B.C. when the Egyptian Pharaoh,

Thutmose III, laid siege to the city for seven months. His victory enabled him to incorporate Canaan as a province in the Empire of the New Kingdom. Six letters sent by Biridiya, King of Megiddo, to the Egyptian Pharaoh Akhenaten in the 14th century B.C. were discovered in the archive of el-Amarna in Egypt. The letters indicate that Megiddo was one of the strongest cities in Canaan.

The Bible lists the King of Megiddo among the Canaanite rulers defeated by Joshua in his conquest of the Promised Land. (Joshua 12:21) According to I Kings 9:15, King Solomon rebuilt Megiddo along with Hazor and Gezer. Many other historical records could be produced to show that this city has had a place of importance throughout history. It will appear in the headlines at least one more time when the greatest battle that has ever been fought will occur in this Valley of Armageddon.

Revelation: Chapter 17

Revelation 17:1-18, "(1) And there came one of the seven angels which had the seven vials, and talked with me, saying unto me, Come hither; I will shew unto thee the judgment of the great whore that sitteth upon many waters: (2) With whom the kings of the earth have committed fornication, and the inhabitants of the earth have been made drunk with the wine of her fornication. (3) So he carried me away in the spirit into the wilderness: and I saw a woman sit upon a scarlet colored beast, full of names of blasphemy, having seven heads and ten horns. (4) And the woman was arrayed in purple and scarlet color, and decked with gold and precious stones and pearls, having a golden cup in her hand full of abominations and filthiness of her fornication: (5) And upon her forehead was a name written, Mystery, Babylon The Great, The Mother Of Harlots And Abominations Of The Earth. (6) And I saw the woman drunken with the blood of the saints, and with the blood of the martyrs of Jesus: and when I saw her, I wondered with great admiration. (7) And the angel said unto me, Wherefore didst thou marvel? I will tell thee the mystery of the woman, and of the beast that carrieth her, which hath the seven heads and ten horns. (8) The beast that thou sawest was, and is not; and shall ascend out of the bottomless pit, and go into perdition: and they that dwell on the earth shall wonder, whose names were not written in the book of life from the foundation of the world, when they behold the beast that was, and is not, and yet is. (9) And here is the mind which hath wisdom. The seven heads are seven mountains, on which the woman sitteth. (10) And there are seven kings: five are fallen, and one is, and the other is not yet come; and when he cometh, he must continue a short space. (11) And the beast that was, and is not, even he is the eighth, and is of the seven, and goeth into perdition. (12) And the ten horns which thou sawest are ten kings, which have received no kingdom as yet; but receive power as kings one hour with the beast. (13) These have one mind, and shall give their power and strength unto the beast. (14) These shall make war with the Lamb, and the Lamb shall overcome them: for He is Lord of lords, and King of kings: and they that are with Him are called, and chosen, and faithful. (15) And he saith unto me, The waters which thou sawest, where the whore sitteth, are peoples, and multitudes, and nations, and tongues. (16) And the ten horns which thou sawest upon the beast, these shall hate the whore, and shall make her desolate and naked, and shall eat her flesh, and burn her with fire. (17) For God hath put in their hearts to fulfil His will, and to agree, and give their kingdom unto the beast, until the words of God shall be fulfilled. (18) And the woman which thou sawest is that great city, which reigneth over the kings of the earth."

This is the chapter that convinces many that a revived or a revised Roman Empire is the setting for much of the book of Revelation, and that the Pope and the Catholic Church play a major part in what is taking place. Rome is a city set on seven hills. There is an interesting Scripture in I Peter 5:12-13. "(12) By Silvanus, a faithful brother unto you, as I suppose, I have written briefly, exhorting, and testifying that this is the true grace of God wherein ye stand. (13) The church that is at Babylon, elected together with you, saluteth you; and so doth Marcus my son."

Notice that Peter mentioned the church in Babylon. Peter wrote his epistle between 64 and 68 A.D. while he was in Rome. Ancient Babylon's last claim to fame, if you wish to call it that, is an accidental one. Alexander the Great died there in 323 B.C. The city's downfall is directly related to the Greek conquest of this region. In 312 B.C., Seleucus founded a new Mesopotamian capital city and named it Seleucia. It was farther to the north on the Tigris River rather than on the Euphrates River. Much of the building material was brought from Babylon which became a forgotten city until it was excavated in the 20th century. The Babylon that we are so familiar with from the Old Testament did not even exist during the time that Peter wrote his Epistle. So, what does he mean when he talks about the church in Babylon? He's talking about Rome. Nero is in power, and Nero hates

Christianity. This was during the time when Christians were fearful for their lives, and they were having to hide and live in the catacombs. They not only had the issue of safety to consider, but they also had the issue of hatred of all things that pertain to God. Peter likened the corruption in Rome unto the corruption of ancient Babylon.

We saw in Revelation 13 the assembling of the unholy trinity. The dragon, the beast and the false prophet came together as imitations of the true Trinity: the Father, Son and Holy Ghost. But there is one thing that is still missing. What is it? It's the church. Since the devil is copying everything else that God does, he has to have himself a church. After the rapture, followed with the beginning of the Tribulation, there are going to be a lot of empty church buildings all over the world. Since the Antichrist sets himself up as Christ, he is able to deceive many into believing that he is either the Messiah who they've been waiting for, or he is Christ who has returned. You have all these empty buildings so the devil just moves his followers in. Since we are now operating under a world system, there has to be a headquarters. Where will that be? How about Rome?

Revelation: Chapter 18

Revelation 18:1-24, "(1) And after these things I saw another angel come down from heaven, having great power; and the earth was lightened with his glory. (2) And he cried mightily with a strong voice, saying, Babylon the great is fallen, is fallen, and is become the habitation of devils, and the hold of every foul spirit, and a cage of every unclean and hateful bird. (3) For all nations have drunk of the wine of the wrath of her fornication, and the kings of the earth have committed fornication with her, and the merchants of the earth are waxed rich through the abundance of her delicacies. (4) And I heard another voice from heaven, saying, come out of her, My people, that ye be not partakers of her sins, and that ye receive not of her plagues. (5) For her sins have reached unto heaven, and God hath remembered her iniquities. (6) Reward her even as she rewarded you, and double unto her double according to her works: in the cup which she hath filled fill to her double. (7) How much she hath glorified herself, and lived deliciously, so much torment and sorrow give her: for she saith in her heart, I sit a queen, and am no widow, and shall see no sorrow. (8) Therefore, shall her plagues come in one day, death, and mourning, and famine; and she shall be utterly burned with fire: for strong is the Lord God who judgeth her. (9) And the kings of the earth, who have committed fornication and lived deliciously with her, shall bewail her, and lament for her, when they shall see the smoke of her burning, (10) Standing afar off for the fear of her torment, saying, Alas, alas that great city Babylon, that mighty city! for in one hour is thy judgment come. (11) And the merchants of the earth shall weep and mourn over her; for no man buyeth their merchandise any more: (12) The merchandise of gold, and silver, and precious stones, and of pearls, and fine linen, and purple, and silk, and scarlet, and all thyine wood, and all manner vessels of ivory, and all manner vessels of most precious wood, and of brass, and iron, and marble, (13) And cinnamon, and odours, and ointments, and frankincense, and wine, and oil, and fine flour, and wheat, and beasts, and sheep, and horses, and chariots, and slaves, and souls of men. (14) And the fruits that thy soul lusted after are departed from thee, and all things which were dainty and goodly are departed from thee, and thou shalt find them no more at all. (15) The merchants of these things, which were made rich by her, shall stand afar off for the fear of her torment, weeping and wailing, (16) And saying, Alas, alas that great city, that was clothed in fine linen, and purple, and scarlet, and decked with gold, and precious stones, and pearls! (17) For in one hour so great riches is come to nought. And every shipmaster, and all the company in ships, and sailors, and as many as trade by sea, stood afar off, (18) And cried when they saw the smoke of her burning, saying, What city is like unto this great city! (19) And they cast dust on their heads, and cried, weeping and wailing, saying, Alas, alas that great city, wherein were made rich all that had ships in the sea by reason of her costliness! for in one hour is she made desolate. (20) Rejoice over her, thou heaven, and ye holy apostles and prophets; for God hath avenged you on her. (21) And a mighty angel took up a stone like a great millstone, and cast it into the sea, saying, Thus, with violence shall that great city Babylon be thrown down, and shall be found no more at all. (22) And the voice of harpers, and musicians, and of pipers, and trumpeters, shall be heard no more at all in thee; and no craftsman, of whatsoever craft he be, shall be found any more in thee; and the sound of a millstone shall be heard no more at all in thee; (23) And the light of a candle shall shine no more at all in thee; and the voice of the bridegroom and of the bride shall be heard no more at all in thee: for thy merchants were the great men of the earth; for by thy sorceries were all nations deceived. (24) And in her was found the blood of prophets, and of saints, and of all that were slain upon the earth."

In Revelation 18, all is coming to a close. We see the destruction of the great city of Babylon and the response of the sinners who have been deceived into thinking that the Antichrist was their savior. They weep and mourn, but heaven rejoices for God has avenged His saints just as He promised He would. As was mentioned previously, there are times in all of our lives when we wonder if the righteous will ever be vindicated. God has promised us in His Word that He will avenge wrongs done to us by the enemy. As we progress through the last days, we see that all those who chose to side against God are truly on the losing side. They boasted of their wealth, their fame, their strength and their power, but all of that is coming to an end. Only the things of God will remain. Evil men rise to positions of prominence for a time, but their end has been foretold. When we read through Revelation perhaps, we should concentrate more on the victory that is assured us rather than all of the things that we will never understand until we get to heaven. I suspect that when we finally get to heaven, we won't care at all about most of the things that occupied so much of our time and attention on this earth.

Revelation: Chapter 19

Revelation 19:1-10, "(1) And after these things I heard a great voice of much people in heaven, saying, Alleluia; Salvation, and glory, and honour, and power, unto the Lord our God: (2) For true and righteous are His judgments: for He hath judged the great whore, which did corrupt the earth with her fornication, and hath avenged the blood of His servants at her hand. (3) And again they said, Alleluia And her smoke rose up for ever and ever. (4) And the four and twenty elders and the four beasts fell down and worshipped God that sat on the throne, saying, Amen; Alleluia. (5) And a voice came out of the throne, saying, Praise our God, all ye His servants, and ye that fear Him, both small and great. (6) And I heard as it were the voice of a great multitude, and as the voice of many waters, and as the voice of mighty thunderings, saying, Alleluia: for the Lord God omnipotent reigneth. (7) Let us be glad and rejoice, and give honour to Him: for the marriage of the Lamb is come, and His wife hath made herself ready. (8) And to her was granted that she should be arrayed in fine linen, clean and white: for the fine linen is the righteousness of saints. (9) And he saith unto me, Write, Blessed are they which are called unto the marriage supper of the Lamb. And he saith unto me, These are the true sayings of God. (10) And I fell at his feet to worship him. And he said unto me, See thou do it not: I am thy fellowservant, and of thy brethren that have the testimony of Jesus: worship God: for the testimony of Jesus is the spirit of prophecy."

These first ten verses are aptly called the "Alleluia Chorus". Do you realize that chapter 19 of Revelation is the only place in the entire Bible where you find the word "alleluia"? At least, that is the case in the King James Version? The definition of the word "alleluia" is "praise God," or more correctly, "I will praise the Lord." When you apply the definition of the word "alleluia", you will find the idea many times throughout the Bible. But in this one chapter, you have the four "alleluias" of the Bible. The redeemed of all ages along with all of creation begin to praise and worship God. Can you imagine what this is going to be like? I mentioned this earlier, but it applies even more so here. If loud worship makes you uncomfortable, you will probably feel out of place in Revelation chapter 19. Praise is going to strike like lightning and roll like thunder throughout heaven, and it will have the sound of many waters. When I stood next to Victoria Falls in Zimbabwe, the site was majestic and the sound was almost deafening. Heaven is going to be more so as it reverberates with thunderous shouts of praise and worship to God.

And then, it's supper time. Have you ever tried to imagine what this is going to look like? Most of us have been to church homecomings or banquets where some type of celebration was occurring. They are joyful and happy occasions. In 1925, a banquet was held in Olympia, London. It is said that they had 5 miles of tables, and 1,300 waitresses were needed to serve 8,000 Freemasons. On September 7, 1995, a wedding reception in India reportedly had over 150,000 guests. But all of these earthly celebrations will be like a drop of water in the ocean compared to this heavenly celebration. While no description is given of this supper in the Bible, the impression we get is that the saints of all ages will be present. I have made my reservation, how about you?

Revelation 19:11-16, "(11) And I saw heaven opened, and behold a white horse; and He that sat upon him was called Faithful and True, and in righteousness He doth judge and make war. (12) His eyes were as a flame of fire, and on His head were many crowns; and He had a name written, that no man knew, but He himself. (13) And He was clothed with a vesture dipped in blood: and His name is called The Word of God. (14) And the armies which were in heaven followed Him upon white horses, clothed in fine linen, white and clean. (15) And out of His mouth goeth a sharp sword, that with it He should smite the nations: and He shall rule them with a rod of iron: and He treadeth the winepress of the fierceness and wrath of Almighty God. (16) And He hath on His vesture and on His thigh a name written, King Of Kings, And Lord Of Lords."

When Jesus came the first time, He came as a baby. He was born in Bethlehem, wrapped in swaddling clothes and placed in a manger. He came to bring salvation. When Jesus comes the next time, He will come riding a white horse as a conquering warrior bringing the armies of heaven with Him. He will bring judgement. Salvation the first time; judgement the second.

Revelation 19:17-21, "(17) And I saw an angel standing in the sun; and he cried with a loud voice, saying to all the fowls that fly in the midst of heaven, Come and gather yourselves together unto the supper of the great God; (18) That ye may eat the flesh of kings, and the flesh of captains, and the flesh of mighty men, and the flesh of horses, and of them that sit on them, and the flesh of all men, both free and bond, both small and great. (19) And I saw the beast, and the kings of the earth, and their armies, gathered together to make war against Him that sat on the horse, and against His army. (20) And the beast was taken, and with him the false prophet that wrought miracles before him, with which he deceived them that had received the mark of the beast, and them that worshipped his image. These both were cast alive into a lake of fire burning with brimstone. (21) And the remnant were slain with the sword of Him that sat upon the horse, which sword proceeded out of His mouth: and all the fowls were filled with their flesh."

Somewhere between verse 19 and verse 20, the Battle of Armageddon is won. We are not given many of the details of this battle. We are told only that the battle starts, Jesus wins, and the enemies of our Lord are cast alive into a lake of fire that burns with brimstone. It looks like the worst is over, but not yet.

Revelation: Chapter 20

Revelation 20:1-3, "(1) And I saw an angel come down from heaven, having the key of the bottomless pit and a great chain in his hand. (2) And he laid hold on the dragon, that old serpent, which is the Devil, and Satan, and bound him a thousand years, (3) And cast him into the bottomless pit, and shut him up, and set a seal upon him, that he should deceive the nations no more, till the thousand years should be fulfilled: and after that he must be loosed a little season."

In chapter 19, we saw that the beast and the false prophet were both cast into the lake of fire. Chapter 20 begins by telling us that Satan is bound and cast into a bottomless pit for 1,000 years. The mental image of this event is that Satan is continually falling for 1,000 years. The unholy trinity has been dealt with, at least for a season.

Revelation 20:4-6, "(4) And I saw thrones, and they sat upon them, and judgment was given unto them: and I saw the souls of them that were beheaded for the witness of Jesus, and for the word of God, and which had not worshipped the beast, neither his image, neither had received his mark upon their foreheads, or in their hands; and they lived and reigned with Christ a thousand years. (5) But the rest of the dead lived not again until the thousand years were finished. This is the first resurrection. (6) Blessed and holy is he that hath part in the first resurrection: on such the second death hath no power, but they shall be priests of God and of Christ, and shall reign with him a thousand years."

As has been stated previously, the idea that no one can be saved during the Tribulation is not true, but it will not be a pleasant time to live. Here in verse 4 we see that indeed people did choose to live for Jesus during this time, but they were beheaded for making that choice. I'm thankful that God's grace reaches into this terrible time even if the cost of postponing what could have been done earlier is going to be high.

There are two resurrections mentioned in the Bible. The first resurrection is for the believer, and it comes before the Millennial Reign. The second resurrection is for the sinner, and it comes after the Millennial Reign. What great rejoicing there will be at the first resurrection. What great anguish there will be at the second.

Revelation 20:7-8, "(7) And when the thousand years are expired, Satan shall be loosed out of his prison, (8) And shall go out to deceive the nations which are in the four quarters of the earth, Gog, and Magog, to gather them together to battle: the number of whom is as the sand of the sea."

After a thousand years, Satan is loosed, and he begins to deceive people again. Let me voice what I have heard others ask, and to be honest, what I have asked myself. I know God has a reason for everything He does and I'm certainly not questioning God, but I don't understand why the devil is given another chance to deceive people. Just look at how many he is able to deceive. Their number is like the sand of the sea. That is a lot of people. I heard a minister make this baseball analogy which I personally think is a little too trivializing. However, it does serve to illustrate a point that we may never understand. When Satan rebelled against God at some point in the dateless past, he was cast out of heaven: strike one. When Satan was defeated at the Battle of Armageddon: strike two. When Satan was defeated at the Battle of Gog and Magog: strike three and he's "out".

Revelation 20:9, "(9) And they went up on the breadth of the earth, and compassed the camp of the saints about, and the beloved city: and fire came down from God out of heaven and devoured them." Unlike the events during the
Tribulation, the judgement here is swift. Fire comes down from heaven and destroys those who have joined with Satan in this rebellion.

Revelation 20:10, "(10) And the devil that deceived them was cast into the lake of fire and brimstone, where the beast and the false prophet are, and shall be tormented day and night for ever and ever." We are finally rid of the devil. He is cast into the lake of fire where the beast and the false prophet are, and we won't ever have to worry about him again. That's a great reason to shout!

Revelation 20:11-15, "(11) And I saw a great white throne, and Him that sat on it, from whose face the earth and the heaven fled away; and there was found no place for them. (12) And I saw the dead, small and great, stand before God; and the books were opened: and another book was opened, which is the book of life: and the dead were judged out of those things which were written in the books, according to their works. (13) And the sea gave up the dead which were in it; and death and hell delivered up the dead which were in them: and they were judged every man according to their works. (14) And death and hell were cast into the lake of fire. This is the second death. (15) And whosoever was not found written in the book of life was cast into the lake of fire."

Notice verse 12. "And I saw the dead, small and great, stand before God; and the books were opened: and another book was opened, which is the book of life: and the dead were judged out of those things which were written in the books, according to their works." There have been all kinds of books written and movies made of this event, trying to imagine what it will be like. The Book of Life is mentioned here not for the possibility of one's name being found but to show the sinner that his name is not there. This is the Great White Throne Judgement. This is not for the saint. This is for the sinner. Their names are not going to be found in the Book of Life.

There are an unknown number of books that contain a record of what the sinners has done and the legal record which shows that they never accepted Christ as their Savior. What a sad and tragic moment! We tend to think of this moment in eternity as a time when just those who were blatant sinners are going to be judged. But in Matthew 7:21-23, speaking of this day of judgement, Jesus carries it a step farther. "(21) Not everyone that saith unto Me, Lord, Lord, shall enter into the kingdom of heaven; but he that doeth the will of My Father which is in heaven. (22) Many will say to Me in that day, Lord, Lord, have we not prophesied in Thy name? and in Thy name have cast out devils? and in Thy name done many wonderful works? (23) And then will I profess unto them, I never knew you: depart from me, ye that work iniquity." On that day, it's not going to matter who my Mama and Daddy were. It's not going to matter how much I may have accomplished in the name of ministry. It's not going to matter how many religious positions I held. What will matter is my relationship with Jesus. Is my name in the Lamb's Book of Life?

The Apostle Paul once made a statement that always causes me to stop dead in my tracks and search my heart. 1 Corinthians 9:27, "But I keep under my body, and bring it into subjection: lest that by any means, when I have preached to others, I myself should be a castaway." Judgement Day is not a day to be taken lightly. Let me reiterate a great

Bible truth found in 2 Peter 3:9. "God is not willing that any should perish, but that all should come to repentance." Ezekiel 33:11 tells us that "God gets no pleasure in the death of the wicked." God has no desire that anyone should perish, but God will not condone sin.

Everyone seems to have an opinion as to what hell will be like. In Matthew 10: 28, Jesus said, "fear not them which kill the body, but are not able to kill the soul: but rather fear Him which is able to destroy both soul and body in hell." I preached a sermon many years ago that I entitled, "The Day Hell Ceases to Exist." Near the beginning of that message, I stated that sinners would not spend eternity in hell. Well, that got everyone's attention. I based my statement on Revelation 20:14. "And death and hell were cast into the lake of fire." Eternity for the sinner will be spent in the lake of fire where Satan, the beast, and the false prophet are. Through the years, you occasionally hear someone boast about going to hell. If hell is just a fraction of what is described in the Bible, it is not a place that anyone should want to go.

Revelation: Chapter 21

Revelation 21:1, "(1) And I saw a new heaven and a new earth: for the first heaven and the first earth were passed away; and there was no more sea." If you have noticed the massive destruction on this earth as we read through the time of Great Tribulation, you can easily understand why a new earth is needed. All the earthquakes will have permanently marred this earth, not to mention the seas and the rivers being turned into blood, the water becoming bitter and undrinkable, and many other tragedies. The earth needs a major makeover. It happens right here. In my mind, it's a makeover on the order of what this earth was probably like in the Garden of Eden. More beautiful than anything we can imagine.

Revelation 21:2-5, "(2) And I John saw the holy city, new Jerusalem, coming down from God out of heaven, prepared as a bride adorned for her husband. (3) And I heard a great voice out of heaven saying, Behold, the tabernacle of God is with men, and He will dwell with them, and they shall be His people, and God Himself shall be with them, and be their God. (4) And God shall wipe away all tears from their eyes; and there shall be no more death, neither sorrow, nor crying, neither shall there be any more pain: for the former things are passed away. (5) And He that sat upon the throne said,

Behold, I make all things new. And He said unto me, Write: for these words are true and faithful."

In the words of a great old hymn, "What a day, glorious day that will be." All of the pain, the sorrow, the grief, the death and the tears that were the result of the fall in Genesis chapter 3 will be gone forever! That's shouting ground! In Genesis chapter 1, we saw the beginning of this earth as we now know it. A history that will have covered about 7,000 years in total by the time we reach this point in the Bible. But in Revelation chapter 21 there will be a new beginning that will have no end.

Revelation 21:6-27, "(6) And He said unto me, It is done. I am Alpha and Omega, the beginning and the end. I will give unto him that is athirst of the fountain of the water of life freely. (7) He that overcometh shall inherit all things; and I will be his God, and he shall be My son. (8) But the fearful, and unbelieving, and the abominable, and murderers, and whoremongers, and sorcerers, and idolaters, and all liars, shall have their part in the lake which burneth with fire and brimstone: which is the second death. (9) And there came unto me one of the seven angels which had the seven vials full of the seven last plagues, and talked with me, saying, Come hither, I will shew thee the bride, the Lamb's wife. (10) And he carried me away in the spirit to a great and high mountain, and shewed me that great city, the holy Jerusalem, descending out of heaven from God, (11) Having the glory of God:

and her light was like unto a stone most precious, even like a jasper stone, clear as crystal; (12) And had a wall great and high, and had twelve gates, and at the gates twelve angels, and names written thereon, which are the names of the twelve tribes of the children of Israel: (13) On the east three gates; on the north three gates; on the south three gates; and on the west three gates. (14) And the wall of the city had twelve foundations, and in them the names of the twelve apostles of the Lamb. (15) And he that talked with me had a golden reed to measure the city, and the gates thereof, and the wall thereof. (16) And the city lieth foursquare, and the length is as large as the breadth: and he measured the city with the reed, twelve thousand furlongs. The length and the breadth and the height of it are equal. (17) And he measured the wall thereof, an hundred and forty and four cubits, according to the measure of a man, that is, of the angel. (18) And the building of the wall of it was of jasper: and the city was pure gold, like unto clear glass. (19) And the foundations of the wall of the city were garnished with all manner of precious stones. The first foundation was jasper; the second, sapphire; the third, a chalcedony; the fourth, an emerald; (20) The fifth, sardonyx; the sixth, sardius; the seventh, chrysolyte; the eighth, beryl; the ninth, a topaz; the tenth, a chrysoprasus; the eleventh, a jacinth; the twelfth, an amethyst. (21) And the twelve gates were twelve pearls: every several gate was of one pearl: and the street of the city was pure gold, as it were transparent glass. (22) And I saw no temple therein: for the Lord God Almighty and the Lamb are the temple of it. (23) And the city had no need of the sun, neither of the moon, to shine in it: for the glory of God did lighten it, and the Lamb is the light thereof. (24) And the nations of them which are saved shall walk in the light of it: and the kings of the earth do bring their glory and honour into it. (25) And the gates of it shall not be shut at all by day: for there shall be no night there. (26) And they shall bring the glory and honour of the nations into it. (27) And there shall in no wise enter into it any thing that defileth, neither whatsoever worketh abomination, or maketh a lie: but they which are written in the Lamb's book of life."

"It is done." Since we are passed the Great White Throne Judgement when we reach chapter 21, verses 7 and 8 almost seem like a footnote reminder of who will and who will not be part of the new heaven and the new earth. "(7) He that overcometh shall inherit all things; and I will be his God, and he shall be My son. (8) But the fearful, and unbelieving, and the abominable, and murderers, and whoremongers, and sorcerers, and idolaters, and all liars, shall have their part in the lake which burneth with fire and brimstone: which is the second death." Verse 27 of this chapter sums it up beautifully when it says, "And there shall in no wise enter into it any thing that defileth, neither whatsoever worketh abomination, or maketh a lie: but they which are written in the Lamb's book of life."

As to the city itself, artists have tried to capture what the New Jerusalem is going to look like, but I don't think our wildest imagination can conceive just how beautiful and majestic it's really going to be. 1 Corinthians 2:9 seems to bear that out. "Eye hath not seen, nor ear heard, neither have entered into the heart of man, the things which God hath prepared for them that love Him."

We are not going to need the sun or the moon any longer for there will be no more night. We are told that there will be people continually coming in and out of the city to worship and honor God. While the city does have gates, they will never be closed. For those of us who grew up during a much simpler time, we remember what it was like when we were kids. No one locked their door, and the windows were always open. Heaven is going to be like that. It will be a safe haven but on a far grander scale. It's going to be 1,500 miles long, 1,500 miles wide, and 1,500 miles high. That's somewhere around 2 million square miles. In a city that is 1,500 miles high and has different stories with twelve feet between each story, you would have almost 600,000 stories. Contrast that with the tallest building in the world, the Burj Khalifa building in Dubai, United Arab Emirates. That is a measly 160 stories and 2,716 feet tall. The New Jerusalem is going to be 3,000 times taller. The wall of the New Jerusalem is going to be about 200 feet thick. It's going to be a sight to behold.

Revelation: Chapter 22

And now, the final chapter: Revelation 22:1-2, "(1) And he shewed me a pure river of water of life, clear as crystal, proceeding out of the throne of God and of the Lamb. (2) In the midst of the street of it, and on either side of the river, was there the tree of life, which bare twelve manner of fruits, and yielded her fruit every month: and the leaves of the tree were for the healing of the nations."

There were two trees mentioned in the Garden of Eden. One was the tree of the knowledge of good and evil. God told Adam and Eve that they could not eat of this tree, but they did. As a result of their disobedience, this world was plunged into sin. We've been dealing with the consequence of that ever since. There was another tree in the Garden of Eden. It was the tree of life. They could have eaten from this one but chose not to. Boy, did they make a wrong choice. At some point, probably immediately after the fall, God removed the tree of life from this earth, and the next time we see it is in the New Jerusalem.

Revelation 22:3-21, "(3) And there shall be no more curse: but the throne of God and of the Lamb shall be in it; and His servants shall serve Him: (4) And they shall see His face; and His name shall be in their foreheads. (5) And there shall be no night there; and they need no candle, neither light of the sun; for the Lord God giveth them light: and they shall reign for ever and ever. (6) And he said unto me, These sayings are faithful and true: and the Lord God of the holy prophets sent His angel to shew unto His servants the things which must shortly be done. (7) Behold, I come quickly: blessed is he that keepeth the sayings of the prophecy of this book. (8) And I John saw these things, and heard them. And when I had heard and seen, I fell down to worship before the feet of the angel which shewed me these things. (9) Then saith he unto me, See thou do it not: for I am thy fellowservant, and of thy brethren the prophets, and of them which keep the sayings of this book: worship God. (10) And he saith unto me, Seal not the sayings of the prophecy of this book: for the time is at hand. (11) He that is unjust, let him be unjust still: and he which is filthy, let him be filthy still: and he that is righteous, let him be righteous still: and he that is holy, let him be holy still. (12) And, behold, I come quickly; and My reward is with me, to give every man according as his work shall be. (13) I am Alpha and Omega, the beginning and the end, the first and the last. (14) Blessed are they that do His commandments, that they may have right to the tree of life, and may enter in through the gates into the city. (15) For without are dogs, and sorcerers, and whoremongers, and murderers, and idolaters, and whosoever loveth and maketh a lie. (16) I Jesus have sent mine angel to testify unto you these things in the churches. I am the root and the offspring of David, and the bright and morning star. (17) And the Spirit and the bride say, Come. And let him that heareth say, Come. And let him that is athirst come. And whosoever will, let him take the water of life freely. (18) For I testify unto every man that heareth the words of the prophecy of this book, If any man shall add unto these things, God shall add unto him the plagues that are written in this book: (19) And if any man shall take away from the words of the book of this prophecy, God shall take away his part out of the book of life, and out of the holy city, and from the things which are written in this book. (20) He which testifieth these things saith, Surely I come quickly. Amen. Even so, come, Lord Jesus. (21) The grace of our Lord Jesus Christ be with you all. Amen."

For those who carelessly and frivolously take God's Holy Word and rewrite it to suit their sin, they should take heed to verses 18 and 19. God's Word is not something to be tampered with nor changed to conform to the age we live in. God's Word never changes. If we live by it, it will take us safely home.

The curse has been reversed. The tree of life and the water of life are in heaven for us to partake of freely. It is going to be an incredible place. I hope to meet you there!

May the grace of our Lord and Savior, Jesus Christ, be with you all.

VI
APPENDIX
RECOMMENDED STUDY LIST

The Holy Bible
Barclay Study Bible, William Barclay
Biblical Illustrator by Joseph S. Exell
Christian History Magazine, Christian Heritage Inst.
Dake Study Bible, Finis J. Dake
Expositions of Holy Scripture, AlexandeR Maclaren
God's Plan For Man, Finis J. Dake
Handfuls on Purpose, James Smith
Holman Bible Atlas, Thomas C. Brisco
Holman Book of Biblical Charts, Maps and
   Reconstructions, Marsha Smith
Images of the Holy Land, Hanan Isachar
Logos Bible Software by Faithlife Corporation
Manners and Customs in the Bible, V. H. Matthews
Manners and Customs of the Bible, James Freeman
Matthew Henry's Commentary by Matthew Henry
Nelson's Bible Commentary by Thomas Nelson
Nelson's Complete Book of Bible Maps & Charts,
   Thomas Nelson
Nelson's Study Bible, Thomas Nelson
Nicene and Post-Nicene Fathers
Pulpit Commentary, H.D.M Spence
Revelation Expounded, Finis J. Dake
Strong's Concordance, James Strong
The Bible Knowledge Commentary, John F. Walvoord
The New American Commentary, James Brooks
The Treasure of Scripture Knowledge, R.A. Torrey
The Two Babylon's, Alexander Hislop
The Works of Josephus, Flavius Josephus
Traveling In the Holy Land through the Stereoscope,
   Jesse Lyman Hurlbut
Word Pictures in the New Testament, A. Robertson
The Kingdom of the Cults, Walter Martin

Made in the USA
Columbia, SC
09 August 2019